W9-BNF-946

This Incredible Need to Believe

EUROPEAN PERSPECTIVES

EUROPEAN PERSPECTIVES

A Series in Social Thought and Cultural Criticism

Lawrence D. Kritzman, Editor

European Perspectives presents outstanding books by leading European thinkers. With both classic and contemporary works, the series aims to shape the major intellectual controversies of our day and to facilitate the tasks of historical understanding.

For a complete list of books in the series, see pages 117–118

THIS INCREDIBLE NEED TO BELIEVE

Julia Kristeva

Translated by Beverley Bie Brahic

COLUMBIA UNIVERSITY PRESS ♛ NEW YORK

COLUMBIA UNIVERSITY PRESS

Publishers Since 1893

New York   Chichester, West Sussex

Bisogno di credere: Un punto di vista laico © 2006 Donzelli Editore, Roma

Copyright © 2009 Columbia University Press

All rights reserved

Library of Congress Cataloging-in-Publication Data

Kristeva, Julia, 1941–

[Bisogno di credere. English]

This incredible need to believe / Julia Kristeva; translated by Beverly Bie Brahic.

p. cm.—(European perspectives)

Includes bibliographical references and index.

ISBN 978-0-231-14784-2 (cloth: alk. paper)—ISBN 978-0-231-51995-3 (e-book)

1. Belief and doubt.   2. Psychoanalysis and religion.   3. Christianity—Psychology.

I. Title.   II. Series.

BD215.K7513   2009

200—dc22

Columbia University Press books are printed on permanent and durable acid-free paper.

This book was printed on paper with recycled content.

Printed in the United States of America

c 10 9 8 7 6 5 4 3 2 1

References to Internet Web sites (URLs) were accurate at the time of writing.

Neither the author nor Columbia University Press is responsible for URLs that may have

expired or changed since the manuscript was prepared.

CONTENTS

THE BIG QUESTION MARK

(IN GUISE OF A PREFACE)

Dear Frédéric Boyer,

I was troubled when you asked if I would add a few pages to this little book, recently published in Italy[1] at the instigation of my editor and friend Carmine Donzelli and in response to his questions. I'll come back to the "need to believe," that narcotic that makes living easier, for—happy infantile and amorous trauma—it is the foundation of our capacity to be . . . *speaking beings.* What worries me isn't that I'd have to confide to you—here and now—the intimate part of the alchemy that, for me, this paradoxical "need to believe" remains: joy and pain, expectation necessarily disappointed, and anguish nonetheless ever enlightening. No, more fundamentally, and in these somber times when the nihilistic certitude of some encounters the fundamentalist exaltation of others, what worries me is whether the believers, and especially those who believe they don't believe, will be capable of reading into my reflections "a big question mark," as Nietzsche wrote, at the place of "greatest gravity." An exorbitant wager underneath its apparent humility? An impossible wager? Cruel and very long-term?

It seems to me henceforth agreed that Christianity opened the vast field of the sacred to figuration and to literature: to the inner experience that goes from the quest of convulsive communion to the necessity I feel of questioning everything—from the abysses of childhood up to the unknown. This is the consequence—sublime or destructive?—of a "disjunction," says Georges Bataille, that Christianity sanctioned: on the one hand, the putting to death of God, who represented and still represents the only opposable limit to irresistible desire, and, on the other hand, the resurrection of the divine in "perfect moments," "privileged situations," "scalding communions." Paint, make music, tell stories: if your possession of the Holy Grail cannot be mistaken for God, it is its inheritance, its return—a sort of return—even if it grows drunk on profaning him.

Faced with that continent we now call *sublimation*, intelligence, in a hurry, has done its best to limit reason to a calculating kind of consciousness: knowledge, as a result, has grown disinterested in inner experience, even going so far as to ignore its intrinsic authority.

For my part, like others but differently, I want here to take a step to one side: neither sublimatory intoxication nor controlling appropriation. An emotional, experiential, and sharable knowledge of the inner experience is possible: it is discursive, it rests upon psychoanalytic transference and takes the form of a theoretical hypothesis by definition ongoing and incomplete. Sigmund Freud's invention of the unconscious, and his interpretation of the "free association" offered him by his patients have rehabilitated—*unbeknownst* to the Viennese doctor?—the authority of inner experience. In confronting *Being* with the death drive, or even Kant with the Marquis de Sade, Freud's successors have started to shake up the phenomenology of the "person" so as to locate the "speaking subject" at the crossroads of biology and the senses. They even go so far—how rash!—as to dispossess theology of its "thing" [*sa "chose" meme*].

However, whatever the clinical advances of psychoanalysis and the theories of signification that it inspires, these are still far from attaining the level to which they aspire and can only hope to do so if the elucidation of the experience in transference and countertransference is heedful of the results of research in the life sciences, in philosophical discourse, sublimatory practices, and . . . religious experience—as Freud was, from the start. Not so as to constitute a new "absolute knowledge," but so that no data, confirmation, or model comes along to put a halt to the questioning, this endless prolongation of the *access to the sacred* that Christianity made possible—in a unique way because infinitely renewable. For modern humanism and the methodologies it forges, this will involve accessing psychosomatic experience in what makes of it a singular life, an ongoing rebirth, an unpredictable creativity.

That, from this point of view, faith be analyzable does not necessarily imply a method for getting by without it—although this too may be. The questioning of any and all entities, including belief and its objects, is one of Christianity's most impressive legacies; and humanism, its rebellious child, must not be prevented from developing this legacy. Are not the legitimate fears caused by secularization, all in all, negligible compared with the vitality of this other direction that inward experience now takes? I speak, as you will have gathered, of the inner experience from Freud on, that which is concerned to elucidate itself so as to deepen and diversify its advances, while taking care not to drift off course. We must not allow the "clash of religions" to lead us to the kinds of identity tensions that might block the way that Bataille, the author of *Atheological Summa*, described thus: "To no longer want to be all things is to call everything into question."

It is in this spirit that I hear, as you invite me to, Saint Paul's well-known statement in 2 Corinthians 4:13—"I believed, and so I spoke"—which for you resonates with certain pages of *This Incredible Need to Believe*. No doubt about it: you are still the subtle reader I praised in the days when you were writing your doctoral thesis on

"The Spiritual Experience in Dostoyevsky and Proust"—to which we must add the perspicacious editor you have since become! But what have I to contribute to what you already know, what your readers hear all the time, and what so many illustrious commentators have revealed to us?

"Credi, propter quod locutus sum," says the Latin text, echoing Psalm 116:10: "Credidi, etiam cum locutus sum: 'Ego humiliatus sum nimis.'" "Epistevsa dio elalisa," says the Greek text, going back to the Greek translation of Psalm 116 in the Bible: "Epistevsa dio elalisa." The Hebrew says: "He'emanti ki adaber . . . "; "I had faith even when I said: / 'I am greatly afflicted' / I who said in my consternation: 'Every man is a liar!'"

The context of the psalm is more explicit: it associates the faith (*emuna*, in which one hears the root *amen*, faith or belief) that governs the enunciation with precise, ordinary, and, as it turns out, deceptive declarations. Faith holds the key to the act of speech itself, even should it be plaintive (I am afflicted, men lie, etc.). Because I believe, I speak; I would not speak if I didn't believe; believing in what I say, and persisting in saying it, comes from the capacity to believe in the Other and not at all from existential experience, necessarily disappointing. But what is: "to believe"? The Latin *credo* goes back to Sanskrit *sraddhā*, which denotes an act of "confidence" in a god, implying restitution in the form of divine favor granted to the faithful; it is from this root, secularized, that *credit* in the financial sense comes: I deposit some good in expectation of reward (Emile Benveniste has meticulously argued this development). In Greek, the etymologies of *pistevo* and *pistis* trace "confidence" in god back to "obedience" to the divine. I won't be telling you anything you don't already know if I say that it is not uncommon to see "contrary meanings," according to modern judgment, expressed by the "ancients" using the same word: because these words bear the mark of the passionate emotional and sensory ambivalences proper to human behavior.

The psychoanalytical experience of the child and the adult, which restitutes the metamorphoses of our personal as well as our phylogenetic evolution from within, testifies to a crucial moment of development, when the *infans* projects itself onto a third person with which it identifies: the loving father. Primary identification with the father of individual prehistory, the dawn of the symbolic triad [*tiercité*] that takes the place of the fascination and the horror of the dual mother-child interdependence, this confident recognition granted me by the father loving the mother and loved by her, and that I in turn grant him, turns my babble into linguistic signs whose value he establishes.

Signs of objects, but above all the signs of my jubilations and my terrors, of my early experience of a living speaking being, they transform my anguish into a "believing, waiting": *gläube Erfarung*, writes Freud. Loving fatherly listening gives meaning to what would be, without it, an unspeakable trauma: nameless excess of the pleasures and pains. But it is not I who construct this primary identification, and it is not the loving father who imposes it upon me either. The *Einfühlung* with him—this zero degree-ness of becoming One with the third person—is "direct and immediate," like a bolt of lightning or an hallucination. It is through the intermediary of the sensibility and the discourse of the mother loving the father a mother to whom I still belong, from whom I am still inseparable—that this "unification" of me-in-the-other-who-is-a-third is impressed upon and founds me. I don't speak unless I am supported by my "believing, waiting" addressed to the loving father of the individual prehistory: this other of the mother, loving the mother no less than the mother/ woman in me, and who has the "attributes of both parents"—this father who was already there, who had to be there, before Laius was, before the from-that-time-forth famous "oedipal" father came along and formulated his laws and prohibitions. Nodes of differences between sexes and generations; and launch pad of identities, of the freedom to make sense.

A myth, you think? More like a novelistic reconstruction that I tell myself along with some Freud embroidering more or less unconsciously on Psalm 116 and Saint Paul's Second Letter to the Corinthians 4:13? Not only.

We say, somewhat glibly, that each of us speaks our "maternal language." Winnicott researched the conditions that make it possible for the mother's and baby's coexcitation to turn into language: he concludes that a "transitional space" is necessary. For example, the reverie of the mother, or a third object between her and the infant, but which object? We had forgotten that Freud himself, that atheistic Jew, that man of the Enlightenment, had sketched, without dwelling on it, this "believer" destiny of the father of *the primary identification* (*The Ego and the Id*, 1923). An imaginary father who, in recognizing me and loving me via my mother, implies that I am not her but other, who makes me believe that I can "believe." That I can identify with him—Freud even uses the verb invest. Believe and/or invest, not in him as "object" of need and desire (this will come later; for the moment my "object" of need and desire is above all mummy), but in his representation of me and in his words—in the representation that I make for myself of him and in my words. "I believed, and I spoke."

On this basis alone, my need to believe, thereby satisfied and providing me with the best possible conditions for language development, goes hand in hand with another corrosive and liberating capacity: the *desire to know*. Supported by this faith that lets me hear and talk to a loving/loved third person, I burst into questions. You see that I have not forgotten our "big question mark."

Who has not experienced the joyful trance of the questioning child? Still on the border between the flesh of the world and the kingdom of language, he knows with an hallucinatory kind of knowledge that each identity—object, person, himself, the response of the adult—is a constructible-deconstructible chimera. And the child doesn't stop bringing us back to this inconsistency of names and of beings, of being, which no longer terrorizes him but makes him laugh, because he *believes* that it is possible to name, to ask for names. Before this vibrant young Self shuts itself up in the certainties of the ego, that "pure culture of the death drive." And before "I believed and I spoke" is changed into clichés, into "communication," into depression.

Lacan thought psychoanalysis's motto ought to be *Scilicet*: "you can know." Indeed, you can know where babies come from, why it is that you speak, what you say, etc. He forgot to recall that "you can know" if and only if you believe you know, so as to come to know why you *believe*, what you mean by believing, what you believe . . . Catholic as Lacan originally was, he must have believed that this was obvious and that there was no point in dwelling on it. Finally, it seems the time has come to return to this "capital gain" of speech, to what shores it up, which is its *plus-de-jouir* [value-added bliss], he would say, by going back further, right back to the believing . . . From the knowing to the believing, and vice versa, the eternal turnstile of *parlêtre* [speakbeing]. Take the possibility of knowing right back to the need to believe, without renouncing the interrogating of the historical contents of beliefs, their truths: absolute or constructive? Protective or temporary? Illusory, beneficial, or death ridden? Endlessly.

The self, writes Freud, in *The Ego and the Id*, being composed of *verbal traces and perceptions* ("The perceptions are to the ego what the drives are to the id"), this copresence of perception and verbalization henceforth sets itself up as a "region," a frontier "district" between the id and the conscientiousness of the [*conscientiel*] superego, and, because of this, as *the object* par excellence of the cure. The frontier experience of psychoanalysis, neither purely interior nor simply exterior, is supposed to transform into perception/verbalization the mnesic unutterable traces of the *chose seule* [thing alone], of the more or less traumatic excitation, on condition that . . . *transference* occurs—oedipal, in the last analysis. Which means that analytical interpretation—this "theory" that "applies" only as a singular attuned to the incommensurable singularity of each—will always be formulated from an oedipal viewpoint (as we say for the accidents of the paternal function), not to be confused with a formulation reduced to the Oedipus complex.

Up until the closing words of his 1938 apothegm on mysticism, "Mysticism: the dim auto-perception of the realm, beyond the ego, of the id," Freud seemed to think that "speaking in psychoanalysis" can—indefinitely—touch upon the *drives* and as a consequence on the *emotions,* by way of the *sensations.* A testament that should be related to his formula in the *New Lectures* (1932): "perception can conceive (*erfassen*) of the relationships in the depths of the ego and the id." Let's understand: what distinguishes the psychoanalytical cure from the mystical opening is that, in mystics, the ego vanishes in favor of the id, which perceives itself. The mystical raptus is a glimpse (vision) that makes a tear in the verbalization and allows the thing seen, along with the underlying drive, to act in silence. Before Eros returns with language's noise and before the mystic speaks and writes. Analysis, on the other hand, is a process, temporal and interactive, continuously constructing/deconstructing the oedipal bond. I hear your question: what is the specifically psychoanalytical underpinning that distinguishes speech in analysis from esthetic or mystical raptus?

As Freud continued to theorize the death drive, and as narcissism showed itself powerless to block it, the *object relation* appeared as the buttress susceptible to modulate the *undoing* [*déliaison*] that opposes Eros and unleashes the powers of death. By dint of insisting upon the *object* of desire—justly and with reason—we have a tendency to underestimate such fundamentals as the in-depth studies of the Oedipus complex, which Freud introduced as early on as *Totem and Taboo* (1912) and continued to develop until *Moses and Monotheism* (1939): an in-depth study of the symbolic capacity ("I believed and I spoke") with regard to the evolutions of paternity, insofar as paternity is, in the speaking animal, the regulator of destructivity.

It is truly this capacity to signify, this *significance rooted in the destiny of the paternal function*, that Freudian psychoanalysis bequeaths us. By linking what is most intimate to the historical mutations by way of the evolution of family structures and the regulation of reproduction, onto- and phylogenetic significance makes history part of the experience of the psychoanalytic couch.

Freud, who was the least religious man of his century, did not hesitate to postulate, in commenting upon the destiny of the paternity that governs the installation of significance and its accidents, "a high aim in human beings": "Das höhere Wesen in Menschen." Far from betraying any kind of idealist regression, this theorization points to the logic of an *immanentism of transcendence*, which psychoanalysis's founder noticed by means of and in the transference at the heart of the "talking cure" he invented.

Some people, when they are suffocating from not knowing wherefrom they speak and what they believe they are saying, enter psychoanalysis. Speaking in analysis then becomes once more a questioning, which is no longer that of conscience [*conscientiel*], but plunges into the system of language. To the point of destroying the work of language as a system of signs and, along with it, the tyranny of identification with the family triangle's substitutes. Before they rebuild, provisionally, the hardly bearable fragility of the paternal function and the crazy endurance of the maternal vocation.

Analysis renders us capable of new *bonds*: this is what most of those involved in it hope for. I shall say that this bond of which the analysand becomes capable is none other than *the bond of investment in the process of symbolization itself*. For the "object," whatever it may be (sexual partner or friend, professional role, symbolic ideal, etc.), and however optimal it appears, can only endure if the speaking subject–analysand is capable of endlessly constructing-deconstructing its meaning: from the need to believe to the desire to know and vice versa.

Only thus, from morality's proximity to its ancestor, religion, but also to the "sciences of the mind," does speaking in psychoanalysis blaze a new path within the link to the process of signification constitutive of the human. And, I repeat, the better to insist upon it, it is this displacement of the act of speaking with regard to itself, this infinitesimal revolution, constitutive of our practice, that troubles the world. I fear psychoanalysts are not sufficiently skillful in the art of demonstrating this exceptional singularity that consists of "speaking in psychoanalysis" to its best advantage: *I believe that I can know*. All the same, this experience seems to me to be the only one that can—not save us from a culture psychoanalysis reveals to us is a culture of the death drive, but create a distraction from this drive: delay it, go around it, divert it, fully cognizant of what we do and why. Endlessly, solely through the ordeal of language that refines language and renders it sensitive to the unutterable by questioning the very conditions of speech, including the need to believe.

Thank you, dear Frédéric Boyer, for the occasion you have offered me to touch upon a few big questions that vitally concern me, starting with this prepolitical and prereligious need to believe, which constitutes—I repeat—only one of the elements in this complex experience of faith. I must not leave you without expressing my gratitude as well to those at the origin of the texts collected in this book: the Archbishopric of Paris, the editors of *La Croix*, and the publishing houses *Parole et silence*, Donzelli and Bayard.

I send you my very best regards.

Julia Kristeva

This Incredible Need to Believe

THIS INCREDIBLE NEED TO BELIEVE

(INTERVIEW WITH CARMINE DONZELLI)

I am not thinking of a substitute for religion: this need must be sublimated.

SIGMUND FREUD, LETTER TO JUNG, FEBRUARY 13, 1910

Can one speak of the "need to believe" from a secular point of view? For the analysis of this basic phenomenon of human life, I'd like us to begin, not with specifically religious arguments, but with considerations that are more in the domain of anthropology or psychoanalysis.

What a great deal you ask of me! Vast undertaking, to try and come to terms with a need to believe that I call prereligious and which brings us up against neither more nor less than the history of humanity: the speaking being is a believing being. We must take the history of religions into account and take some side trips into anthropology and psychoanalysis . . . a tall order! Furthermore, you invite me to embark on this adventure before this Italian audience, which embodies two thousand years of history, without accounting for what came before that, under the gaze of a Europe that is the bearer of both hope and peril. Fine, I've attached my seatbelt: ready for takeoff! "I travel myself," says Stéphanie Delacourt, the heroine of my metaphysical detective story *Murder in Byzantium.*[1]

Your question makes an appeal to the humanities, today more than ever confronted—beyond their "regional" problems concerning the meaning of discourses—with the challenge of different kinds of fundamentalism and the wars of religion, a challenge that I choose to define, in a somewhat peremptory manner, as a pressing need to radically reform humanism.

I count myself in effect among those who think that in the great crises the West has undergone—particularly during the Renaissance but also in the eighteenth century and, in another way, today—men and women have managed to elucidate and recompose this need to believe with which they were confronted, to one side of and differently from the way religions do. Did the mystics not, right from the outset, attempt such an experiment, in a kind of internal exclusion from the "canon"? More directly, your question reminds me of the humanists of the Renaissance who, beginning with Petrarch, Boccaccio, Ficin, and Pica de la Mirandola, by way of Erasmus, Montaigne, Thomas More, and even Nicolas de Cues, to mention just a few, no more abolished the need to believe than they confused it with that of the established religions. The French Enlightenment and the Encyclopedists—Voltaire, Rousseau, Diderot, right up to and including the scandalous Marquis de Sade—thoroughly studied and radicalized this path, going from deism to atheism.

The "God of the philosophers," need we repeat, gets reduced to the "a priori proof," which rests only on "the fact that something is possible" (Kant). From Parmenides to Leibniz and Heidegger, the "divine" gives way to *being* ("*being* is, *nonbeing* is not"; "why *is there something* rather than *nothing*") and the *subject* thinking in it (in the being; Descartes' "I *think* therefore I *am*"). "White theology" or "apple juice"? The juicy expression is Freud's who, for his part, was to seek another way.

An outgrowth of the dissolution of ontotheology, the humanities in turn have not hesitated to grapple with variations on the religious and the sacred. As early as the end of the nineteenth century, Emile Durkheim examined the elementary forms of religious life, while Marcel Mauss analyzed prayer, the gift, and the sacrifice; closer to our own time the works of Lévi-Strauss have examined myth, those of Mary Douglas impurity . . . on the horizon of these kinds of thinking, is the Freudian discovery of the unconscious and the founding of psychoanalysis that still guides my thought, which I should like briefly to recall as we begin our conversation.

To believe . . . This is not the "I believe" in which I often hear an "I suppose," as in the sentence: "Reading these e-mails, I don't believe he loves me; hearing his voice, I believe he loves me." The "believe" that concerns us today is that of Montaigne, for example, when he writes: "For Christians recounting something incredible is an opportunity to believe" (*Essays*); or the "believe" of Pascal: "The mind believes naturally, and the will loves naturally; so that, lacking real objects, they have to cling to false ones" (*Pensées*, 2.81); or again that of Voltaire: "My interest in believing in something is not a proof of this thing's existence" (*Twenty-fifth Letter on the Thoughts of Monsieur Pascal*). Whether I belong to a religion, whether I be agnostic or atheist, when I say "I believe," I mean "I hold as true."

BELIEF-CREDIT [CROYANCE-CRÉANCE]

What kind of truth are we talking about? Not a kind that may be logically demonstrated, that may be scientifically proved, that may be calculated. It is a matter of a *truth* "we stumble upon," to which I cannot not adhere, that totally, fatally subjugates me, that I hold for vital, absolute, indisputable: *credo quia absurdum*. A truth that keeps me, makes me exist. Rather than being an idea, a thing, a situation, might it be an experience?

If this need "to hold true" is not satisfied, my apprenticeships, convictions, loves, and acts just don't hold up. But what "holds it up," this need to "hold true," this "need to believe"? Is it inevitable that it be religious?

Credo—from the Sanskrit *kredh-dh/srad-dhā*—means "to give one's heart, one's vital force, in the expectation of a reward" and designates an "act of confidence, implying restitution," the act of "confiding something with the certainty of getting it back," religiously (to believe) and economically (credit). Emile Benveniste, in his *Indo-European Language and Society,* insists upon the correspondence between belief [*croyance*] and credit [*créance*]: Vedic man puts his desire, his magic force (more than his heart) in the gods; he puts his confidence in them and counts on getting something back: Indra is the god of help, Sraddhā is the goddess of the offering. Saint Augustine is one of the first to invite us "to read the Scripture with the eyes of the heart fixed upon our heart" (*De Doctrina Christiana,* 4, 5.7). Paradoxically, necessarily, it is a Jewish atheist, Sigmund Freud who, trying plumb the depths of the unconscious, made of the "need to believe" an *object of knowledge.*

A superficial reading of *The Future of an Illusion* (1927) allows us to think that Freud reduced belief to an illusion. An illusion that human beings have a great deal of trouble ridding themselves of, so greatly are they given to swaddling themselves in pleasant fantasies rather than yielding to reason. This line of thought, present in Freud, but whose brief sketch is forever being exceeded by contemporary psychoanalysis, moves in tandem in Freud's own work with multiple advances we are still exploring: from *Totem and Taboo,* the exchanges with Jung, Romain Rolland, or Pastor Pfister, right up to *Civilization and Its Discontents* (1930) and *The Man Moses* (1939).

Furthermore, analytic experience itself is not foreign to "belief" in the broadest sense of this term: does not the transference/countertransference establish, at the heart of the analytical cure, the conviction both affective and logical that the interpretation is well-founded? Add to this the fact that the analyst begins by "believing"

in the psychic reality of his analysands: it doesn't matter if the analysand himself entrusts me with inept phantasms, I begin by believing
in these beliefs, in these apparent absurdities, before we manage in
the long run to dissolve them or at least endlessly and inconclusively
elucidate them. In this overview of belief, I take another step: I integrate the tales, myths, and theories of the analysands in my interpretation, which, from the subjective, purifies itself into something
objective; and, in validating them as states constituent of the psychic
life, I return them to the fields of knowledge and of therapy.

This closeness of psychoanalysis to belief was greatly reproached
him: I'd say even today, in the era of rough sex and its double, Pu-
ritanism, resistance to psychoanalysis is less a matter of the fear of
the "sexual"—which is more and more spectacular and banal—than
of this Freudian incursion into the field of belief. Psychoanalysts have
not failed to notice this, as you can imagine, and several of my French
colleagues (among them especially Sophie de Mijolla-Mellor) have
already devoted colloquia and publications both remarkable and eru-
dite to the similarities/dissimilarities between psychoanalysis and
faith as well as to the various aspects of the "return of the religious,"
be it in the guise of the need to believe, of sects, or of the clashes between religions.

To rapidly sum up the originality of the analytical position, as it
appears one hundred and fifty years after the birth of Sigmund Freud
(1856–1939), let me mention merely a few of the proposals, which
have found precise and substantial clinical and theoretical development in Freud's successors, Melanie Klein, Lacan, or Winnicott.
Thus Freud permits himself to speak ironically about the God of the
philosophers: for him this is all "apple juice"—as I said—"containing
a minuscule percentage of alcohol, or maybe no alcohol at all, but
people get drunk on it all the same" (letter to Marie Bonaparte,
March 19, 1928). One more reason to acknowledge the psychic reality of religious experience, which Freud perceives as a "regressive ar-

chaism" that can be "approached by means of mythology and the development of language" (letter to Jung, February 2, 1910). Although he recognizes the fragility of his "young" science, Freud is persuaded that it is illusory to "receive from elsewhere" what this science cannot give and affirms that he is resolutely enrolled under the banner of "God Logos" in his prospecting of the sacred intoxication; "Our God Logos is perhaps not all-powerful, he may perhaps accomplish but a small part of what his predecessors promised" (*The Future of an Illusion*, 1927).

"OUR GOD LOGOS"

Might this Freudian "god" called Logos be a reminiscence of the Church Fathers? In effect, Tertullian, Clement of Alexandria, and Origen, readers of Plato—who seem to inspire Pope Benedict XVI even today and who steal in under the skeptical pen of our Viennese Jew—profess that the world is organized by God in a rational manner, the believer participates rationally in this world and receives the biblical revelation as well in a rational way. Faith and reason are reabsorbed into "divine reason," a sort of Logos. Tertullian, good Aristotelian that he is, goes so far as to validate improbability since, as Freud would say, the "inept" itself contains a "kernel of truth": *credibile est ineptum*, therefore *credo quia absurdum*? Closer no doubt to Diderot (the only French philosopher he cites), and to his "See God everywhere he is or say that he is not" (*Philosophical Thoughts* 26) or to Spinoza in his *Deus sive Natura*, Freud was persuaded that our "psychic apparatus" (which transforms the libido into images and thoughts) "is itself a constituent part of the world that we must explore and which readily allows such exploration" (*The Future of an Illusion*). This certainty led him to subscribe to the possibility of knowing . . . "our God Logos" himself. It is a matter of scientific knowledge, to be sure, which will nonetheless be a mixture of the imaginary, belief, of the absurd even: "Only sages are ethical solely for the pleasure of reason; others need eternally true myth" (letter to Jung, November 11, 1910). Do you know of any sages without myths? As for the absurdity of beliefs, let us recall the irony of James Joyce who, when asked why he preferred Catholicism to Protestantism, replied: "Why should I renounce a coherent absurdity for an incoherent one?"

THE OCEANIC FEELING . . .

Two mental experiences, corresponding to stages constituent of our "animistic" or "psychic" apparatus, confront the clinician with the *need to believe*. Let me sketch them.

The first goes back to what Freud, in response to a question from Romain Rolland, describes, not without reticence—he feels "uneasy" "disserting on such imponderables"—as the "oceanic feeling" (*Civilization and Its Discontents*). This would relate to the intimate union of the ego with the surrounding world, felt as an absolute certainty of satisfaction, security, as well as the loss of our self to what surrounds and contains us, to a container, and that goes back to the experience of the infant who has not yet established borders between the ego and the maternal body. Indisputable and unsharable, given only to "a few" whose "regression goes sufficiently far back," and nonetheless authenticated by Freud as an original experience of the ego, this prelinguistic or translinguistic experience, dominated by sensations, supports *belief*. Belief, not in the sense of a supposition, but in the strong sense of an unshakable certainty, sensory plenitude, and ultimate truth the subject experiences as an exorbitant kind of more-than-life [*sur-vie*], indistinctly sensory and mental, strictly speaking ek-static. Certain works of art bear witness to this: I have noticed it particularly in Proust. The narrator speaks of dreams without images ("the dream of the second apartment"), woven with pleasures and/or pains that "one" "believes" (he states) unnameable, that mobilize the extreme intensity of the five senses and that only a cascade of metaphors can attempt to "translate": the telling of these dreams may be interpreted as a triumph over the endogenous autism that inhabits the unconscious depths of each of us, according to the psychoanalyst Frances Tustin. Might the writer succeed where the autistic fail? I mean, very precisely, the one who succeeds in naming this boundless immersion of the ego in the world, which, being correctly named, ceases to be a catastrophic abolition of the self, but is felt as an "oceanic feeling," as a jubilant osmosis of the subject in the common flesh of a "not-yet oneself" swallowed up in a "not-yet world." The autistic person, however, does not manage to extract himself from this absence of differentiation between his flesh and the flesh of the world because he cannot represent them. On the other hand, the capturing in language of this belonging of the ego to a container gives rise to a feeling of omnipotence and truth, which is a source of certainty and elation. "A kind of bliss," a friend, who associates artistic inspiration with mystical exaltation, used to say. The need to believe—with the power of its dazzling certainty, its sensory joy, and the dispossession of oneself—might perhaps commemorate this archaic experience and its pleasures and risks.

It seems to me that this is a point that is unfamiliar except to specialists: we don't know much about how Freudian thought, such as you evoke it here, deals with borderline mental states and their management by religion or, in another way, by writing.

True, and Freud himself goes in this direction very cautiously, against his better judgment even. Only modern clinicians have refined our observations about the early dependency of mothers and babies and the impact of this upon the adult psyche, particularly in aesthetic and religious experience. The founder of psychoanalysis declared himself (to Romain Rolland, July 20, 1929) "closed" to mysticism, as to music, but also to Nietzsche's kind of thinking; while avowing, without further precision, the "specifically Jewish nature of *his* mysticism" (to Jung, 1909). Why this relative "closure"? Might it be to protect himself from the maternal feminine? So we suppose, on the part of a nonetheless very courageous explorer into the "black continent" of femininity who, until his final years ("Femininity," 1933, *The Essentials of Psychoanalysis,* 1938)—and the death of his own mother—put off going more boldly in the direction of this "minoemycenian civilization," predating classical Greece, to which he compares the early relations of the little girl with her mother: stormy seas if ever there were any! And that transform women into ardent seekers of faith, into believers often more fervent than men. But also into radical rebels, disappointed beyond consolation, and even into impenitent atheists when they succeed in casting off this hypnosis of the "archaic maternal," to which Irresistible Mister Baby seems more easily to succumb.

. . . AND THE PRIMARY IDENTIFICATION: DIRECT AND IMMEDIATE.

Far from exhausting the complexity of the need to believe, this Freudian plunge into the certainty of me-world, of the ego mingled with the flesh of the world, goes hand in hand with a no less fleeting and suggestive illumination of another element of the need to believe: "I" am only if a beloved authority acknowledges me. That psychoanalysis be based upon the amorous experience reiterated, decomposed, and recomposed in transference/countertransference is something I upheld in my book *Tales of Love* (1987). Within the broad spectrum of love bonds, Freud (*Totem and Taboo*) emphasizes "desire (*Sehnsucht*) for the father": the "murder of the father of the primitive horde," far from extinguishing this desire, only stimulates it, fans the flames, and leads to the establishment of an absolute ideal, which, according to Freud, underwrites the religious feeling. Moreover, and as if to designate the need to believe as the central kernel of a vaster religious feeling, in *The Ego and the Id* (1923) Freud posits a "primitive identification" with the "Father of individual prehistory." "Direct and immediate" *(direkte und unmittelbare)*, this identification anterior to any objective relation of desire is not destined for the oedipal father but for a . . . loving father, who would have . . . the "attributes of both parents." The oedipal father, on his part, object of love-hate, only comes along later to incite revolt and murder as the condition for the appearance of an autonomous and thinking subject.

At the dawn of individuation a life raft thus appears on the horizon of the "oceanic feeling": the loving father. An imaginary Surface who, though his loving authority, takes me from the engulfing container: he is the guarantor my being. This unwonted celebration of the loving Father under the pen of the inventor of the Oedipus complex is depicted as a fleeting emotional identification, "direct and immediate," because the young child doesn't yet have to elaborate it: it is transmitted by the love of the mother for the father of the child and for her own father. A *third party* henceforth infiltrates the archeology of the need to believe: this is an oblative paternity, endowed with a subliminatory capacity that, because its love acknowledges the symbolic being of the newborn, confers upon it the dignity of being. In acknowledging me, the father's loving authority makes me exist. This is a fundamental support, without which I would not be able to achieve any norm, accept any frustration, obey any prohibition, take upon myself any law or moral code. The primary identification is with the basis of the authority, for, constituted by the loving acknowledgment of a third person, it breaks with the terror and tyranny that threaten the powerless premature being of the newborn—and it initiates culture.

On the one hand: the oceanic *Gehfül* that extrapolates maternal dependence from a representation of contained-container and confers upon the ego the jubilant certainty of belonging to the world, the "omnipotence" of "being part of." On the other: the primary identification with the Father of individual prehistory whose loving authority calms the primary anguish and transmits to me the conviction of "being." "I" does not stop seeking these primary constituents of his identity in his incredible need to believe.

PSYCHOANALYSIS AND MYSTICISM: RESEMBLANCE/DIFFERENCE

Up until the end of his life, Freud was to maintain the vis-à-vis between psychoanalysis and mysticism; so as to oppose them, of course! Psychoanalysis aims at "the perception by the ego of the id" (*New Introductory Lectures on Psychoanalysis*), echoing the statement "Where it was, shall I be" ("Wo Es war, soll Ich werden"); whereas Mysticism is the "vague self-perception of the realm, beyond the ego, of the id" (states the ultimate Freudian apothegm of 1938). The path of mystical belief plunges the ego into the id by means of a sort of sensual autoeroticism that confers a kind of omnipotence on the id: revelation and absence, pleasure and nothingness. The analytic cure is addressed to the same pleasurable encounter of ego and id, but allows these two psychic apparatuses to circulate, by means of the transference words, from the id to the ego and back, from the ego to the id. Resemblances? Absolutely. But no confusion! Easier said than done!

I call it *incredible,* this prereligious "need to believe," for it is not a question of making of it an absolute, flattering it and using it as a basis for this or that order or hierarchy—neither is it one of ignoring it, at the risk of mutilating the individual capacity to think and create, at the risk of harming that which does not want the social bond itself to congeal into constraints but to be a bulwark, an optimal condition for democratic debate. Is it not surprising that our secularized societies have neglected this incredible need to believe? By this I mean they deny the necessary paradox that consists in responding to the anthropological need to believe, without reducing it to the historical forms that the history of beliefs confers upon it but by sublimating it (as Freud says) into diverse practices and elucidations.

In thus scrutinizing the foundations of individuation, analytical listening does not claim to lay flat the complexity of religious experiences. It is content to open some perspectives for observations and theorizations that, in allowing a more complex understanding of the psychic apparatus, reveal how much the need to believe is part and parcel of the speaking subject "before" any strictly religious construction and of course within secularization itself. A "site" barely hinted at and whose edification it is our task to pursue. For I am convinced that by taking this prereligious need to believe seriously, we could confront not only religions' past and present fundamentalist off-course drift but also the dead ends of secularized societies. Particularly the incapacity of these to establish some kind of authority, an incapacity that leaves the way clear for violence on the one hand and the automation of the species on the other. How to claim, in effect, to impose an authority in which no one believes if the problematic of belief itself is annulled and if, as a consequence, these "sublimations" that Freud called for are no longer encouraged? Jurists are asked to come up with just solutions to conflicts, including religious conflicts, forgetting that jurisprudence gets its authority from a general consensus on essential moral principles. But it is precisely this consensus that our multicultural and recomposed societies lack, deprived of moral bases because incapable of federating heterogeneous beliefs around mere "human rights," perceived as "abstract." When we attempt to create this consensus now and again in the "political debate," we quickly see that the "democracy of opinion" is wide open to the freedom of judgment of each "quid," of "*who* you are," writes Hannah Arendt, to be differentiated from the "quod," of "*what* you are." The living political bond, understood and practiced as a sharing of creativity, calls upon the singularity of each person: had "one" forgotten this? This brings us back to subjective autonomy, that is, to the preconditions of liberty and/or of individuation, the raw wound of the . . . need to believe. The least one can say is that secularized societies fail to take any of this into account.

If the denial of the need to believe leads to the collapse of authority and the absence of moral foundation, do you agree with those who postulate that totalitarian crimes are induced by the loss of religious feeling? That secularization leads to the Shoah? Perhaps even to this demoralization that fundamentalist religions wish to fight?

I'll come back to the possibility of a link between secularization and Shoah. But, to remain for a few moments in the realm of current events, I should like to come back to your question on the "need to believe" in the light, dare I say, of the fires that have recently devastated some of the outlying neighborhoods [*banlieues*] of French cities. Whatever may be the economic or legal reasons for this crisis, which concerns, at bottom, the failure to integrate adolescents "from immigrant populations," I think the unrest is much more widespread, that it touches adolescents of all social milieus and is related to a very serious denial by secularized societies, which refuse to admit that adolescence is *ill from ideality*. How to make sense of that?

THE ADOLESCENT IS A BELIEVER

The child-king asleep in the "infantile" in each one of us, comes into the world with a "polymorphous perversity" (as Freud writes in *Three Essays on the Theory of Sexuality*, 1905), not to be confused with adult perversion. So seductive is this perversity—for the parents but also for theoreticians of all ilk—that it has come to gloss over the characteristics of the adolescent, who has become the forgotten—or should I say the sacrificed?—category of modern societies. Precisely because there is no such thing as an adolescent without the need to believe.

Shall I expand on this? The polymorphously perverse *child*, still according to Freud, is dominated by drives that are inevitably polymorphous because dependent upon the satisfaction of the erogenous zones, of the primary incestuous relationship (maternal seduction or *mère-version*, and of the ultraprecocious oedipal stumbling block or *père-version*). The tumult of the drives is satisfied and worked through via fantasizing activity in the form of a *denial-Verneinung* ("I don't desire mummy" = "I desire mummy"); in the wake of this negativity identified by Freud, language, with its grammatical and logical synthesis, fashions itself. Thus "armed," the polymorphously perverse child *wants to know* where he comes from: he creates sexual theories in response to his key question "where do babies come from?"

In other words, infantile polymorphism is at the junction of the *autoerotic* drives and a *quest* for some object relation; the polymorphously perverse child is a subject of epistemophilic curiosity, of the wish to know; *the polymorphously perverse child is a seeker after knowledge.*

Nothing of the sort during adolescence, or, more precisely, the "polymorphously perverse seeker" gives way in adolescence to a new kind of subject who *believes in the existence of the erotic object* (object of desire and/or love). He only looks for it because he is sure *it must exist. The adolescent is not a lab scientist; he's a believer.* All of us are adolescents when we are passionate about the absolute. Freud didn't devote much time to adolescents because he himself was the most unbelieving, the most irreligious human ever to live. Faith implies a passion for the object relation: faith is potentially fundamentalist, like the adolescent. Romeo and Juliet are its blazon.

However, since our drives and desires are ambivalent, sadomasochistic, our belief that the *Ideal Object exists* is forever being threatened or even brought up short. Then the passion in search of an object shows its other side, the side of punishment and self-punishment. With, to go along with them and keep the adolescent company, their cortege: namely, disappointment-depression-suicide; not to mention, in a more regressive and somatic mode, the anorexic syndrome; or even, should the political context lend itself, the urge to destroy oneself-with-the-others that I've called the kamikaze syndrome.

Because *the adolescent believes in the object relation, he suffers cruelly from its impossibility.* In effect, during adolescence we idealize the parent-couple while wishing to remake it, only much much better, and as a consequence we belittle and disparage it; we cut ourselves off from it so we can replace it with a new model, promise of absolute satisfaction for the adolescent subject we have become. Thus impelled, the *narcissism* of the ego, tied to its *ideals,* overflows into the ardently sought love object, making room for the *amorous passion* that, with the partner, idealizes the drives and their satisfactions.

Let me sum up: from a biological and cognitive evolution, the polymorphic perverse child is capable of enacting a decisive mutation: this is the junction between his libidinal impulses *and* the phantasm of some absolute libidinal satisfaction, thanks to a new object, onto which he projects his narcissism, shored up by the ideal of the ego: "the object is treated like the ego itself"; in other words, "in the amorous passion an important quantity of the narcissistic libido overflows onto the object" (*Group Psychology of Masses and the Analysis of the Ego,* 1921). This junction between the ego and the object (we are not far from the baby's "oceanic feeling," but henceforth reshaped and rediscovered by the idealizing of the amorous bond) goes hand in hand with the belief of being invested with the duty and the power to surpass the parental couple, and even to abolish it, so as to escape it into an idealized, paradisial variant of total satisfaction. The Judeo-Christian paradise is an adolescent creation: the adolescent takes pleasure in the syndrome of paradise, which may also become a source of suffering, if absolute ideality takes a turn toward cruel persecution. Since he believes that the *other,* surpassing the parental other, not only exists but that he/she gives him total satisfaction, the adolescent believes that the Great Other exists, which is bliss [*jouissance*] itself. The least disappointment in this syndrome of ideality hurls him into paradise's ruins, in the form of punitive behavior. Here the polymorphously perverse child is back, but "under the lash of paradise, that pitiless tormentor," to paraphrase Baudelaire. The innocence of the child gives way to necessarily sadomasochistic satisfactions that draw their violence from the very strictures of the ideality syndrome, which command the adolescent: "Your pleasure shall have no bounds!"

BELIEF AND NIHILISM: THE MALADIES OF THE SOUL

We can understand that, structured by idealization, adolescence is nonetheless a *malady* of ideality: either the adolescent lacks ideality or in a given context his ideality doesn't adapt to his postpuberty drive and the need to share with an absolutely satisfying object. Whatever the case may be, adolescent ideality is necessarily demanding *and* in a state of crisis, all the more so as the drive/ideality pair is forever threatening to come undone. Adolescent belief inevitably goes hand in hand with adolescent nihilism. Why?

Remember that adolescence breaks out of childhood at the very moment the subject is convinced that *there is another ideal for him*—partner, husband, wife, professional-political-ideological-religious ideal—and that this ideality is already present in the unconscious; the adolescent unconscious is structured like this ideality. *There cannot not be an absolutely satisfying other*: such is the faith, the passion of the adolescent unconscious. This phantasm, of course, neither meets the test of reality nor the assault of the drives, which weaken the aforesaid belief or, worse, overturn it. Since *it exists* (for the unconscious), but "he" or "she" lets me down (in reality), I hold this against "them" and I get back at them: vandalism follows. Or, on the other hand, since *it exists* (in the unconscious), but "he" or "she" disappoints or fails me, I have only myself to blame and to take my disappointment out on: mutilations and self-destructive attitudes follow.

This *fanatical belief* in the existence of the absolute partner and total satisfaction *blocks* the movement of the representations between the various psychic registers that characterize what I have called the "open structure" of the adolescent, owing to the relaxing of the superego under the pressure of these desires; and it *stabilizes* the subject. An extremely dangerous stabilization, nonetheless, if it is true that belief, according to Kant, is a "sufficient assent only from a subjective point of view, but which we hold to be insufficient from an objective viewpoint" (*Critique of Pure Reason*, 2.2, chapter 2). One might as well say that a belief is a phantasm of maximal satisfaction and inexorable necessity, *fatal* (a term recurrent in fiction about adolescent passion) for the life of the subject: in other words, halfway between the imaginary scenario that depicts both desire and delirium, belief is not itself delirious but has the potential to become so. The *drive/ideality* amalgam comes apart under the increased force of the drives, and this disintegration augments the potential for delirium. It should not surprise us that, structured by this aptitude for belief, the adolescent is easily carried away by enthusiasm and romanticism to the point of fanaticism. But he is also exposed, not only because of the relaxing of the psychic apparatus but also because of the stimulation of the drives by the ideality syndrome, to the defensive explosion of *speech and acting out that is, in the strictest sense of the word, delirious* and that plunges the subject into schizophrenia.

Now, since the adolescent is the first to believe that an Ideal Object of Love, in capital letters, naturally, exists—since he believes this heart and soul—since he is a mystic of the Love Object, well then the breakdown of the paradisial syndrome, when the phantasm fails to find its way toward a process of sublimation (school, profession, vocation that balances or replaces the Ideal Object of satisfaction), leads inevitably to *depressiveness* in the guise of ordinary boredom: "If I don't have Everything, I'm bored." And makes for punitive types of behavior that are just so many ways of compensating for boredom and are rooted in polymorphous perversity. Here it is back again, whipped up by the pitiless paradisial desire and its punitive modes of behavior. These modes of behavior are, indeed, merely the seamy side of the malady of ideality that persists and supports them, not allowing itself to be shaken and even less abolished.

Drug addiction abolishes consciousness but renders belief in the absolute of orgasmic regression real in a hallucinatory kind of pleasure.

Anorexic behavior breaks with the maternal line, and reveals the battle of the young woman against femininity, but brings about an overinvestment in the pureness-and-hardness of a body, which tends to connect with the phantasm of a spirituality, it too absolute: by this phantasm, the whole body disappears into a Beyond with strong paternal connotations.

A *contrario,* the perpetuation of the paradisial syndrome, notably in the idealization of the *bourgeois couple,* as portrayed by TV soap opera cliché, or by *people* magazine-type glamorizing of the life of the couple, has become a pillar of global morality. These show business, commercial, or vulgar variants upon an excessively secularized paradise are intrinsically religious; they are the visible secular face of the deep need to *believe* that nourishes adolescent culture. It took the recent crisis of ideologies and the Middle East conflict to make this religiosity, now globalized, burst into the light of day, although it has long been inherent in social organization. It has been shown how, since Rousseau notably, the "couple" has become the magic formula destined to create a bifaced subject, at once guarantor of the parent-child bond and of the state-citizen bond: I come back to this in the conclusion of my triptych *Feminine Genius.* The Rousseauian ideal is, to be sure, untenable; but it can only be contested through debauchery, perversion, and crime—this is how Sade unmasked the repressiveness of the "social contract." And it is what adolescent "gore," in its desperate fashion, attempts when the dead end of the paradise complex incites to gang rape or vandalism.

The impregnation of the id with ideality differs from one individual to another and according to family or cultural contexts: we are familiar with the superegolike severity of certain adolescent models, sources of guilt and heroism, as well as with others' absence of reference points, which pushes them to regress or transgress. But, whatever their differences, in all of them the biological clock inexorably sets this particular phenomenon in action, I insist: *the shadow of the ideal has fallen over adolescent drive and crystallized into the need to believe.* The purity of Adam and Eve, Dante's encounter with Beatrice in Paradise, Romeo and Juliet as ideal, because impossible, couple are important clues to this ideality throughout our civilization. And it is not because these mythic remains are in abeyance that they do not go on working upon adolescence underneath the variants modern marketing does its best to impart.

Symbolic Authority Deprived of Credibility

This is where the analyst gets taken in, for he has a tendency to cling to the erotic or thanatic symptom, and overlook the ideality in control of the symptom from the unconscious. How take into account the fact that the adolescent believer's unconscious is constructed as a high-risk ideality?

So-called primitive civilizations had *rites of initiation,* in which, on the one hand, symbolic authority (divine for the invisible world, and political for this world) was affirmed, and during which, on the other hand, so-called initiatory sexual practices took place, permitting acts that would today be considered perverse.

In our Western culture, especially in medieval Christianity, the impact of *mortification rituals as well as excessive fasting* in the anorexic behavior of girls and the sadomasochistic acting out of boys has been noted and made to seem either banal or heroic.

Looking at this in a different way, secular this time—and this strikes me as an imaginary elaboration of the adolescent crisis—I've suggested we consider *the birth of the European novel* takes shape around the character of the adolescent. The young page in the service of the

Lady is the pivotal point of courtly love around which a gamut of homosexual relations, more or less elaborate, is deployed. The novel as genre is constructed around adolescent figures: enthusiastic idealists in love with the absolute, ravaged at the first misstep, depressed or perverse, sarcastic by "nature," eternal believers and as a result perpetually in revolt and potentially nihilist. You know them: from the courtly romance to Dostoyevsky and Gombrowicz, they murmur their *credo*. This is a journey that terminates, in the bourgeois novel, in the stabilization of the couple in marriage's highly provisional *happy ending*. Even today best sellers mine this sort of narrative logic, put in place in the Renaissance, which *rough sex* doesn't make a dent in, into which, quite the contrary, it is easily absorbed.

Compared with other modes of "taking charge of" adolescents, is the psychoanalytic sort of listening cure at all innovative, and, if so, how?

The analyst's job is to hear the adolescent's need to believe and to authenticate it: adolescents come to us to have the existence of their ideality syndrome acknowledged. If we do not formulate and share this acknowledgment, we cannot properly understand and interpret the punitive types of behavior of the acme of adolescents in crisis as a place of extreme pleasure, as a "simili-paradise." Only at a third stage should the analyst venture to indicate the negative value, the oedipal or orestean revolt, of such forms of behavior.

In other words, only the capacity of the analyst to know and recognize the pleasure-seeking, idealizing path taken by adolescent drives allows him to be a credible and efficient site of transference and to metabolize the *need to believe* that he will have shared into the pleasure of thinking, questioning and analyzing. In sharing the syndrome of ideality particular to the adolescent, the analyst may eliminate resistances and help the adolescent along the path to an analytical process that the adolescent is often recalcitrant about.

The religious need, relayed throughout the twentieth century by ideological enthusiasm, has proposed and continues to propose to legitimize the ideality syndrome. It is not by chance that adolescent malaise, which is a source of concern for modern society (to the point of its providing fat subsidies to inaugurate with much pomp this or that Home of the Adolescent), goes along with a return of the religious, very often in bastardized (sects) or fundamentalist (which in the name of ideals encourage an explosion of the death drive) forms. In this context, adolescence may also be an opportunity, if we can reflect upon it in such a way as to better attend adolescents in their need to believe and its mirror image, the impossibility of such belief. We would then be better able to interpret the variants of this new malaise of civilization that surrounds us and is expressed by the return of the "need to believe." And that we take part in through our own eternal adolescence.

Let's return to the crisis, in France, but also elsewhere, of the young who live in "suburban ghettos[banlieues]." Isn't this a failure of the French model of secularism, of laicity?

Is this the fault of the "French model"? Or its dreadful advantage?

Contrary to what some of our closest friends in the world say, not only is France not "lagging behind" in this crisis involving adolescents with roots in the immigrant population, but it is "ahead" compared with analogous situations elsewhere. This even explains why the malaise is felt here as more serious: its roots go deeper.

Although religious manipulation of the pyromaniacs is not to be excluded, and although community-related reflexes ostensibly underlie the need for recognition shown by the incendiaries, the crisis of our "suburbs" is not religious; nor is it aimed a posteriori against "the not-displaying-any-signs-of-religious-affiliation rule." Religious authorities disapprove of the violence; parents do not support their delinquent children; this is not an interethnic and interreligious clash as it was in other countries. Everybody firmly denounces the failure of the processes of integration to which these youth aspire; the objects torched are symbols of envy: cars, supermarkets, warehouses—so many marks of "success" or "wealth," so many "values" for relatives and adults—schools, crèches, police stations, so many marks of a social and political authority they wish to be part of. Do people want to destroy secular and republican France when they boo the minister of the interior, only yesterday so popular? Do they mean to attack Christianity when they set fire to a church? "Blogs" invite us to "fuck France" in a rage of excitement without any clarifying discourse, any program, any demands. On the political level, this need of ideals, of recognition and respect crystallizes into a single battle, and it is a huge one, considering the suffering it reveals and the extent of the changes needed: the battle against discrimination.

AFTER AND UNDERLYING THE "CLASH OF RELIGIONS"

Is the "clash of religions" yet to come? Are our adolescent pyromaniacs unable to clothe their need of ideality in religious dress? Some would have it so and go so far as to point their finger once more at French secularism, which stands accused of having done away with the guardrails of religion. I don't share this opinion. *I think that the delinquency of "disadvantaged teens" reveals a more radical phase of nihilism, a phase that comes along after and goes deeper than the "clash of religions."* This kind of delinquency is more serious because it grapples at a deeper level with the inner workings of civilization in this prereligious need to believe that is constituent of the psychic life with and for others that we are trying, in today's conversation, to highlight. This is where parents, teachers, and intellectuals are called upon. While politicians must be pragmatic and generous, it is up to us to propose ideals adapted to modern times and to the multicultural soul.

Adolescent nihilism abruptly reveals that henceforth religious treatment of the revolt is discredited, useless, incapable of assuring the paradisial aspiration of this paradoxical believer, this nihilistic believer, necessarily nihilist because pathetically nihilist, this disintegrated adolescent, cut off from society in the pitiless global migration. Indignant, we reject him—unless he threatens us from within.

The French Republic faces a historical challenge: can it deal with the crisis of belief religion no longer keeps the lid on that affects the very foundations upon which human bonds are built? The anguish paralyzing the country at this decisive moment is an expression of its uncertainty before the size of the stakes. Are we capable of mobilizing all the means at our disposal, police as well as economic, not overlooking those who offer their knowledge of the soul, in order to accompany with the necessary, fine-tuned listening process, with appropriate education and with generosity, this poignant malady of ideality expressed by our outcast adolescents that threatens to submerge us?

Put in these terms, the "French crisis" cannot not concern you. I have tried to tell you how it concerns me and how it concerns the intellectual as I understand her or him. Am I optimistic—too optimistic? I prefer to define myself as an energetic pessimist who only appreciates intelligence active in its thinking processes, or the actuality of the intelligence.

How do you see the growing power of religions today?

I have just emphasized the denial of the prereligious and prepolitical need to believe in secularized fields of knowledge and ideologies. How not also recall, above all, the various political and religious manipulations the world powers have employed in their desire to dominate globalization, which have fanned the flames of dormant fundamentalisms? Show business society, for its part, encourages hypnotic regression and drunken emotionality, along with the calculating kind of thinking that predominates as technology expands, to the detriment of critical thinking, to a questioning kind of thought. However, and much closer to my own area of expertise, let us question the responsibility of the social sciences, and the humanism that inspires them, in this "growing power of religion" that you point to.

Relaying theology and philosophy, the social sciences have replaced the "divine" and the "human" by new objects of investigation: social bonds, kinship structures, rituals and myths, the life of the psyche, and the genesis of languages and works. We have acquired unprecedented knowledge of the richness and risks of the human mind, and this knowledge is unsettling, it encounters resistance, provokes censure. Still, promising as they may be, these territories fragment human experience; the heirs of metaphysics, they keep us from discovering new objects of investigation. The intersections between these compartmentalized domains do not by themselves suffice as bases for the necessary new humanism. Right from the start the thinking subject must get involved in the world, by an affective, political, and ethical "transference." My work as a psychoanalyst, the writing of my novels, my interventions in the social domain are not "engagements," but arise from this mode of thinking that I seek and that I conceive of as an *energeia* in the Aristotelian sense: a thought in action, the actualizing of the intelligence.

Furthermore, the interpretation of texts and behavior, notably— for my part—in light of semiology and psychoanalysis, allows a new approach to the religious continent. The discovery of the unconscious by Freud has shown us that, far from being "illusions," though all the while being illusions, the different beliefs and kinds of spiritualities accommodate, encourage, or make use of precise psychic movements, which allow the human being to become a speaking being, a seat of culture or, inversely, of destructiveness. To take only a few examples, I shall evoke the importance of the law, the celebration of the paternal function, or the role of maternal passion in the sensory and prelinguistic support of the child. My work as an analyst has convinced me, furthermore, that when a patient embarks upon the analytical experience, he comes to ask for a sort of pardon, not in the sense of the effacing of his misery, but in the sense of a psychic and even physical rebirth. It is the possibility of this new beginning, made possible by transference and interpretation, that I call a *par-don* [*by-gift*]: to give and give oneself a new time, another self, unforeseen bonds. We are now able to recognize the complexity of the inner experience that faith cultivates, but also to flush out the hate beneath the appearance of the loving discourse along with the death drive used for purposes of political vengeance or in pitiless wars.

Another conception of the human is therefore being constituted thanks to the contributions of these new *Humanities* in which we share, where transcendence is immanent. This conception is called desire of sense and is itself inseparable from the pleasure that has its root in sexuality and that controls the sublimity of culture as well as the brutality of acting out.

Clearly the intellectual today faces a difficult, historic task worthy of the crisis of civilization: the task is neither more nor less than to help this new type of knowledge gradually emerge. To make use of technical terms unhesitatingly, but without getting locked into their significations, always too narrow. In positioning ourselves at the interface of diverse "disciplines," we may have a chance to elucidate, even in a small way, that which remains enigmatic: psychosis, sublimation, belief and nihilism, passion, the war between the sexes, maternal madness, murderous hate.

A RADICAL REFORMATION OF
HUMAN EXISTENCE IS UNDERWAY

I hear your question: is there still a place for this knowledge in a world caught in a vise between the wars of religion and technology?

After noting that totalitarianism was the end of rationalist humanism in the twentieth century, and announcing that economic and biological automation would be the end of the species in the twenty-first century, two distinguished interlocutors, Joseph Ratzinger and Jürgen Habermas, recently got together to declare ("Prepolitical

Foundations of the Democratic State") that our modern democracies are disoriented because they lack a trustworthy "higher" authority, the one thing capable of regulating the mad dash toward liberty. This convergence of philosopher and theologian gives us to understand that a *return to faith* is the last chance, our one and only possibility, face to face with the perils of liberty, of creating some sort of moral stability. In other words, since constitutional democracies need some "normative presuppositions" on which to base "rational law," and since the secularized state has at its disposition no "unifying bond" (Böckenförde), they suggest the necessity of constituting a "conservative conscience" that will be nourished by faith (Habermas) or that will "provide a correlation between reason and faith" (Ratzinger).

As a counterpoint to this hypothesis, I would like to suggest that we are already confronted, in advanced democracies in particular, with experiences that render null and void any call for a "normative conscience" and the reason/revelation duo, given that advanced democracies are already well on their way to a radical reformation of the humanism of the *Aufklärung* without any recourse to the irrational. It is precisely at this sensitive point of modernity that the literary experience is located—and the theoretical thinking from which it cannot be separated—and the Freudian discovery of the unconscious. I am aware, we are aware, that their respective contribution to the increasing complexity of Enlightenment humanism remains insufficiently perceived, in its pre- and transpolitical scope, as being capable of forming the "unifying bond" that secularized political rationality lacks. Such, however, is the hypothesis—an alternative to the chorus of Böckenförde/Habermas/Ratzinger—that I defend in my writing, and here today.

Contrary to what some would have us believe, the clash of religions is but a surface phenomenon. The problem of this beginning of the third millennium is not the war of religions but the rift and void that now separates those *who want to know that God is unconscious* and those who would rather not know this, the better *to enjoy the show that proclaims He exists.* Global media, with all their imaginary and financial resources, support the latter preference: not wanting to know anything, the better to revel in the virtual. In other words: *get pleasure out of seeing promises and be content with the promises* of goods, guaranteed by the Promise of a higher Good. This situation, because of the globalization of the denial that goes along with it, is unprecedented in the history of humanity. Saturated with seductive and deceptive initiatives, our television civilization shows itself propitious to belief. And in this way it encourages the return and *revival* of religions.

Nietzsche and Heidegger warned us: modern man suffers from "the absence of a sensual and supersensual world with the power of obligation." This annihilation of divine authority and, along with it, any other authority, state or political, does not necessarily lead to nihilism. Nor to its symmetrical opposite, which is fundamentalism up in arms against impiety: in making the *divine* a *value,* even the "supreme value," the transcendentalists link up with nihilistic utilitarianism. But how to know this today without deluding oneself with a narrowly rationalist humanism or a romantic spirituality?

I claim that the alternative to the rise of religiosity, as to its opposite, narrow-minded nihilism, comes already from precisely those *thought loci* that we are attempting not to occupy but to bring to life. Who *we?*

We whose attachment to the vast continent of the social sciences comes from our involvement in languages and literature. Literature, writing, constitute an experience of language that cuts across identities (sexual—*gender*—national, ethnic, religious, ideological, etc.). Whether they be in league with or hostile to psychoanalysis, literature and writing work out a risky kind of knowledge, singular and sharable, concerning the desire for sense rooted in the sexual body. In doing so, literature—writing—shake up the metaphysical duo *reason versus faith,* around which scholasticism was formerly constituted. They invite us to shape an interpretive, critical, and theoretical discourse that follows up upon the advances in the human and social sciences and has the capacity to involve the interpreter's own subjectivity. How?

Those who are open to experience through literature and, in a different but related fashion, open to psychoanalytic experience—or who are merely attentive to what is at stake in these kinds of experience—are aware that the reason/faith or norm/liberty opposition is no longer tenable if *the speaking being* that *I* am ceases to think of himself as dependent on a supersensible world and, even less so, on a sensible world "with the power of obligation." They are also aware that this *I* who speaks unveils himself to himself inasmuch as he is constructed in a vulnerable bond with a strange *object* or an ek-static *other,* an ab-ject: this is *the sexual thing* (others will say: the object of the sexual drive whose "carrier wave" is the death drive). This vulnerable bond *to* and *within* the sexual thing—which underpins and shores up the social or sacred bond—is none other than the heterogeneous bond, the very borderline between biology and sense on which our languages and our discourses depend, which are modified by it or, running counter to it, modify the sexual bond itself.

In this way of understanding the human adventure, literature and art are no more an aesthetic decor than philosophy or psychoanalysis claim to bring salvation. But each of these experiences, in their different ways, offer themselves as laboratories of new forms of humanism. Understanding and accompanying the speaking subject in his bond with the sexual thing allows us to confront the new barbarities of automation, without falling back on the sorts of guardrails that infantile conservatisms hold up, and freed from the shortsighted idealism with which trivializing and on-its-last-gasp rationalism likes to delude itself.

Yet if the venture that I sketch here, attuned to literature and the human sciences of the twentieth century, allows us to predict a recasting and even a radical reformation of humanism, putting this into operation and the consequences of so doing can only be, to paraphrase Sartre, "harsh and long-term."

I belong to the generation that objected to soft humanism, this fuzzy "idea of man," devoid of substance, bonded to a utopian fraternity, which harked back to the Enlightenment and the postrevolutionary contract. Today it seems to me not just vital but possible to refashion these ideals, for I am convinced that what we call modernity, so often disparaged, is a crucial moment in the history of thought. Not hostile to religions, and even less indulgent with them, this school of thought that I am part of is perhaps our last chance to deal with the rise of obscurantism and its other face: the management via technology of the human species.

It is probably even more difficult in the United States than it is in Europe to plead for the reformative role that the "Humanities" might play in a social and political field threatened with disintegration, such as we experience it, differently but similarly, in all the countries of the world today. Still, I plead, not only because this conviction underpins and shores up my own intellectual endeavors but also because I am convinced of the necessity to be aware of it, proudly aware, and in this way counteract the depressive temptation that can overcome the researcher, the intellectual, the writer in this empire of calculation and show business. And also to shout out the need for a more courageous sort of participation, more appropriate to the general public, in this "democracy of opinion" that modern showbiz society has become.

You speak of the literary experience, and yet very often in your writing you criticize in harsh terms the turning-into-merchandise or fetishizing of works of art, whether they be literature, painting, or film . . . Yet you seem to accord a large place to "genius" and its potential for "revolt." Might this not be a new kind of . . . religious . . . hope? Something akin to the quest for an unspoken and unconscious community with a universal will that transcends us?

The notion of "genius" brings with it, in our civilization, a genealogy whose richness will lead me, I hope, to clarify the sense in which I make use of it today. And perhaps even what Freud had in mind when he said that it wasn't so much a question of "founding a religion" as "sublimating" the need to believe.

ORIGINAL GENIUS AND "GREAT MEN"

It is probably unnecessary to recall to Italian readers that the Greek *daimon* to begin with and Latin *genius* later on evoke a "particular god" who watches over each man, thing, place, state. This "presence of a god" from birth, sharing the destiny of the "being" and disappearing with him, translates from the start an intrinsic communion between the divine and the human, an *ingenium quasi ingenitum*, a "sort of divine inspiration" (Voltaire was to say) consubstantial with the human being in ancient ontotheology. Genius is therefore an *encounter* (between *this* human and *his* god) that comes to constitute the specific *singularity* of humans in the Greek, Jewish, and Christian tradition: that which is singular, or particular, is envisaged from the outset as a kind of copresence of the human and the divine. A sign of exception or of inaugural election, an incommensurable caesura, such a "coming to earth" of the divine is vested in a specific temporality: it cuts through the homogeneous flow of time, it breaks up the usual chronological experience, which is without representation, precisely by inserting into it the space of a signification, of a destiny. Genius is, in this sense, a *kairos* that cuts, incises, and inscribes in the cosmic and vital flux, an expanse of sharable stories, of acknowledgment, of memory. Henceforth *zoē* becomes a *bios,* and that which we must call the "originary *genial* encounter" possibly prefigures a heroic destiny. With which to found, at the same time, the political temporality, which is only possible as an articulation of particular caesuras, potentially or in practice heroic.

Later on (allow me this giant step!), when the Gospels proclaim the "good news" of the Parousia, of the *presence* of the Messiah following the *resurrection,* the bond with the divine, such as Saint Paul proclaims it, is expressed as faith: *pistis.* Let's leave aside the question of whether the Gospel *faith* is contrary to biblical *law,* or whether (as I might argue, as others before me) it returns to and reaffirms the holiness and goodness of that law. What concerns me today, with regard to genius, is the recasting of the singularity of the "encounter with genius." The Christian faith's "justice" is linked to its quality of love: "faith works through love" (Galatians 5:6), which is to say that in Christianity henceforth the copresence between human and divine is to be a gift of love, received and given back, that in its very gratuitousness fulfills a promise and brings into being a pact, thus tracing the outlines of the optimal space for a social and historic exchange. The "singularity" of genius, in the "originary" sense of the term, in this case implies the *putting into action* of the divine, proclaimed ("evangelized") presence, which is the presence of love of and for the Other. Faith is an *energeia,* an intelligence set going by love (*agape*), which is the same as saying that the New Alliance demands subjective acknowledgment. The singularity of originary Greek and Latin *genius* is somehow absorbed into *the singular experience of the love of God.* It pushes into Christianity's orbit this loving desire to surpass oneself found in both the "anybody" who earns respect for his living being and in the excesses of saintliness, knightly heroism, or the art that goes into the construction of cathedrals. I consider this self-surpassing as a fulfillment of Jewish messianism. But perhaps it is the *haecceitas* of Duns Scotus that best sums up the absorption of the ancient quality of genius into the genius (!) of Christianity.

We must wait for the Renaissance, as Hannah Arendt noted, for men, who were losing God, to displace transcendence toward the best among them. Frustrated to see themselves assimilated to the fruits of their activities, even the most grandiose, the subjects of galloping secularization endeavored to confer the traits of the "genius" and/or the divinity within each of them upon the producers of matchless works of art. By metonymy, the divine is displaced, unless it vanishes into the person who has the quality of "genius," or simply exercises an influence. The man of genius (there is no question of women) becomes an exceptional but nonetheless sharable singularity: innovative, a carrier of an irreducible excess and, despite this, or rather thanks to this, paradoxically recognized as useful because productive at the heart of social activities. Does this "modern" reinvention of genius already show a refusal to let oneself be reduced to the status of "product" or "appearance" in a society of "consumpation" and "entertainment"? Doubtless, for some. An appeal to the aristocracy of the elite, in reaction against plebeians or the rise of democracy? Is the "great man" the eternal return of the divine, finally [enfin], the final [enfin] version of the divine as Nietzsche's reconstruction of the Superman at the turn of the twentieth century implies?

I distinguish, therefore, in the history of European genius that I have just broadly sketched, between, on the one hand, an "originary encounter with genius" crystallized in the ontological *haecceitas* and made manifest in Jewish and Christian singularity and, on the other hand, the secularized metonymy of the genius of the "great men," prominent from the rebirth of humanism right up to Romanticism.

THE DEBT OF THE HUMAN SCIENCES
TOWARD ONTOTHEOLOGY

The uncertainties of secularization in our time reopen this recurring problematic in a new way. The remains of the ontotheological continent, too rapidly decreed sunk, seem less and less like "dead letters" and more and more like laboratories of living cells whose exploration might allow us to clarify present aporias and impasses. Faced with the trivialization of discourses, with the collapse of authority, with the technical specialization of fields of knowledge that renders their excellence noncommunicable, and with the flood of avid needs of seduction-satisfaction-annulment, the word *genius* is still a hyperbole that arouses our capacity for *astonishment:* that last detonator of thought. I take up the word *genius* again, therefore, but endeavoring to extract it from its romantic inflation. Once again I mention its *archeology*, its sense from before the fetishism of the Renaissance, setting between parentheses for now the idea of "great men" upon which Hegel meditates in his *Lectures on the Philosophy of History:* "The great men of history are those whose particular ends enfold those large issues that are the will of the universal genius." In the three volumes of my *Feminine Genius: Arendt, Klein, Colette,* "genius" must be understood as arising from the *loving singularity* discovered by Christianity, which has since seen some unexpected developments both in what we term the history of arts and letters and in the Freudian discovery of the unconscious.

When the "human sciences" (anthropology, sociology, linguistics, literary theory, psychoanalysis) fragmented the human experience, they rendered null and void its global treatment via ontotheology by introducing new and precise kinds of knowledge: but in censoring the fact that these came from the continent from which they were cutting themselves off, the human sciences limited the scope of their inquiry, as I've just said in response to your previous question. Rhetoric, linguistics, grammar: yes, but on what "language object"? With what debt to the "logos"? To the "logos" of the Stoics, of Plato, of Aristotle, of the Sophists? To the *modi significandi* of the medievals, to the Grammar of Port-Royal, to Sensualism, to historic and general linguistics . . . etc? The talking subject: yes, but *ego cogito* or *ego amo*? A thinking subject or a believing subject?

Still largely invisible and nonetheless at work, it is to my way of thinking the Freudian discovery of the unconscious, as read and interpreted by Lacan, that lets us rethink this copresence of the signifying energy, of *signification* through love, in the singularity of the human adventure. This discovery opens a new page in the "philosophy of immanence" (which I would trace back, with Y. Yovel, to Spinoza) that allows the reconsideration of the old question of *singularity* and *genius* that concerns us today. Isn't the aim of the cure, precisely, to reveal to the analysand his own particular singularity, thereby encouraging the creativity that seems to be the best criterion for ending analysis?

At the height of "structuralism," I was among those who sketched out a current of thought since termed *poststructuralist*: into the structuralists' semiotic and linguistic considerations, this current integrated the *subject of the enunciation* with its bonds to the other and to history (*The Revolution in Poetic Language*, 1984). The extraordinary creative singularity of "great men" (Mallarmé, Lautréamont) seemed to me inaccessible unless one kept in mind the Freudian discovery of the unconscious, which, for its part, is audible only if one approaches language not as a *code*-object of linguistics, but as an "amorous discourse" (with the understanding that the analytic transference actualizes, along with the traumas, the cruel dynamics of infantile and adult amorous experience and lays subjectivity open to its risks as well as to its creative possibilities; to its constitutive geniusness). Lautréamont could only encourage me in this iconoclastic exploration of the quality of genius, with his highly politically incorrect rage against the "big mushy heads" as he called Intellectuals: "Despite our illusions of greatness, which have us by the throat, we have an instinct that corrects us, that we can't repress, that elevates us!" "One says solid things, when one isn't trying to say extraordinary ones." "I want fourteen-year-old girls to be able to read my poetry." "Poetry must be made by all. Not by one. Poor Hugo! Poor Racine! Poor Coppée! Poor Corneille! Poor Boileau! Poor Scarron! Bling, blang, blong!" This is about as far as one can get from "faith"? In effect, but also very close to what I shall call its accomplishment in *haecceitas* as "intelligence moving through love": through *eros* and *agape,* of course, but without for a moment forgetting their carrier wave of hate, destructivity, all of this recomposed in the dynamics of sublimation.

To put it another way, I understand and practice psychoanalysis (clinically or in my interpretive essays) as one of the *adventures of immanence. Infinite intellectual love,* realized also in other "significant practices" (literature, art, etc.) when they are carried out and received not as "objects of consummation" but as the very being of the active intelligence and the plenitude of loving experience. I have, therefore, been led to approach its variants and accidents in the analytic cure, but also in literary texts, as demonstrated in the triptych *Powers of Horror* (1982), *Tales of Love* (1987), and *Black Sun* (1989).

SURPASSING THE SELF IN THE
IMPUDENCE OF ENUNCIATION

Each time and in the three directions taken by these books: whether it be the story of love bonds (narcissism-idealization); of ab-jection (uncertainty of the limits between subject and object, notably in psychosis, phobias, or marginal cases); or of depression or melancholy (clinical or in its literary and artistic manifestations), I am just as interested in the original genius of all subjectivity as in that of the "great works of art" recognized by the cultural "canon."

This is where your question about the meaning of *genius* and *works of art* with regard to the new religiosity acquires meaning. We must describe and analyze the *logic,* not of the *product,* but of the *productivity,* with as much precision as the different "disciplines" allow or, better yet, the *logic* of, for example, the conscious and unconscious dynamics of Marcel Proust's *In Search of Lost Time.* We must bring out the specific and the extraordinary aspects of this text and this experience, while indicating how and why they are intelligible, accessible to the "genius" of the ordinary reader. For without these sharable logics of *creation* and *reception,* the "great man" in the Renaissance—and Hegel's—sense quite simply doesn't happen. It is this "community" of the partakers in the creative experience that interests me, rather than that, hypothetical, of the "great men" or of the "religious experience." For example?

Ironic and vengeful, Colette claimed not to have known any of "the men other men call 'great.'" I myself wouldn't say that, for I recognize in myself one virtue: astonishment, which is not, as you know, counted among the "theological virtues." Consequently, the extraordinary inventiveness of the men and women I meet always impresses me, including the most modest among them, the handicapped even. But it literally subjugates me to meet those whose experience is newsworthy—that is, it makes me happy.

On the other hand, I wouldn't say that there is a "tacit and unconscious community" among these geniuses, rather that each of them— Shakespeare or Darwin or Einstein, all of whom were of interest to Freud—brings subjective experiences and discoveries that respond to universal preoccupations, those likely to be *encountered* by other creative subjectivities, in the infiniteness of time. These encounters depend, evidently and each time, as much on the bio-psycho-social capacities of individuals as on the historical and political context of their reception. Thus the genius of Freud did not *receive* that of Voltaire or Tchouang-tseu, while Mishima, on the other hand, was receptive to that of Saint Sebastian.

My reading of singularity (originary genius) and of genius (in the Renaissance and Romantic sense of the term), which I shall describe, once more, as a tributary of a philosophy of immanence, which interprets loving intelligence beginning from the Freudian unconscious, associates genius both with those disasters of subjectivity called depression and melancholy and with pre- or translinguistic activities, in which this *sense* is engaged with *drives* and *sensations*. Proust's or Colette's "sensory time" could not manifest itself in its *singular genius* or in its *"genial" greatness* unless we were capable of reading the text as a tactile, gustatory, olfactory, oral, visual *experience* along with and beyond its verbal construction: a carnal experience associated with the flesh of the world, as Merleau-Ponty, in his own way, has suggested.

Sublimation, in these authors but also in others, grasps the dimension of meaning that I call semiotic, within and beyond the limits of the "symbolic" order imposed upon us by the kinds of signification proper to language as system of signs. At the crossroads between *semiotic* and *symbolic,* and via this "impudence of enunciation" that is style, sublimation communicates to the reader the impact of a perception, triggering the effect of a contact with the real. An illumination even. Or an "oceanic feeling."

Might this partaking, of each one of us, in the genius of the "great men and women" rehabilitate, in our present culture, the *self-surpassing* that both antiquity and the Jewish and Christian religions or, in yet another way, the "genius" of the "great men," encouraged? The spectator of the global era is fascinated by shocking images and complains only of the dearth of "great men" the better to denigrate them, to "deconstruct" them or ignore them, if by some miracle these manage to make themselves heard over the hubbub of banality. All that remains to us of the "great leaders and teachers" is nostalgia, or a fleeting glimpse, or a virtual apparition—which sometimes astound us, with such telegenic performances that we project our fleeting ideals and enthusiasms beyond the project and to no avail. The mirror and its narcissistic consolations seem to have replaced the *encounter of beings* and existence, as well as reverence for the peerless singular, in others and oneself. Faced with this unprecedented stifling of the need to believe, the mirage of the Superman appears to us a grandiose promise, but we know it is in vain that we would resurrect the cult of "the great." I'm willing, however, as you have seen, to bet that, confronted with the absence of fixed criteria capable of founding "values," the intelligence of the extreme singularity (as manifested in exceptional works of art, for instance) that *calls out to the singularity of each one of us,* is the only possible therapy for this banalization.

Yet you insist, both in your work as an analyst and in your interpretation of the facts of modern culture, upon depression as one of the main signs of our era: black sun of melancholy on the analyst's couch, national depression in face of migratory fluxes, narrowing of the novel into what you call "the minimalism of the self," which, in its narcissistic display, hopes to cure depression and even nihilism. Nor does depression spare women.

Much more than to depression, it is to a crisis of identity, akin to psychosis, that the twentieth century, with the tragedy of its two world wars, with the Shoah and the Gulag, was exposed. In this context I have tried to come to terms with a major difficulty, still far from being resolved: how to speak of a dazzling stylistic achievement, "a work of genius" if you will, when it is permeated with delirium to the point of being imbued with Nazi ideology? Such is the dilemma posed in particular by the work of L. F. Celine. This dilemma shatters the good old romantic notion of "genius" and invites us to analyze in detail the psychic cleavages of the author, their contagious effects upon the reader, the political context, the national cultural tradition, the cathartic, or, on the contrary, the inciting role of "literary magic," the resources of phantasmic and verbal seduction, and so on. My book, *Powers of Horror: An Essay on Abjection* (1982), arose from these questions, broadly outlined, which some of my students are still pursuing.

Is there a feminine genius?

How not to be aware that the twentieth century was forced to admit, under the pressure of various kinds of feminism, the existence of *feminine* genius, once all too easily reduced to maternal devotion and manual work? The three volumes of my *Feminine Genius* (2001– 2004) come in the wake of what has preceded and should also be read as a response to the kind of feminism that I call massifying. Against "all women" and against the "community of women"—for, in the wish to eliminate the question "to be" or "not to be" by the safety of belonging, it was considered desirable to compact women, as the community of the bourgeois, of the proletariat, of the third world, and so forth, once saw themselves compacted. I seized upon the provocative term *genius* to show that I am not really "feminist" but . . . "Scotist." I ask myself questions about singularity, as I've said, according to Duns Scotus's formula and I attempt to analyze it concretely in Arendt, Klein, and Colette. Of course, depression also arises in such cases, as in men, and the inaugural book on melancholy that is attributed to Aristotle already diagnosed it in all men of genius. Indeed, unless I am in mourning for the loss of the usual objects of satisfaction, day-to-day ties, banalized kinds of language, why would I attempt to reconstruct *myself* by reconstructing the *bond*, which is, as I have said, of necessity an amorous bond, at the same time as it is a bond of meaning? For it is undoubtedly this reconstruction, beyond mourning and melancholy, that might hold the promise of a surprising, singular, a "genial," achievement.

So, is there a feminine genius that might have escaped Pseudo-Aristotle?

In original genius, as in the extraordinary genius of these three women, I note to begin with a few specific traits of female psychosexuality in general. Far from being as narcissistic as people say and, on the whole, less narcissistic than men, women are straightaway involved in relationships with others: to live means to live for the other, including, and above all, when this is impossible and traumatizing. Far from locking themselves into the obsessional palace of pure thought, thinking, for women, cannot be shut off from carnal sensoriality: the metaphysical body/soul dichotomy is, in these women, unbearable; they describe thought as physical happiness, *eros* for them is not dissociable from *agape* and vice versa. Their time is necessarily punctuated by a concern for finitude, but without being haunted by the race to death, and it is calmed by the miracle of birth, a kind of opening out. *To be reborn has never been impossible for me*; Colette's exorbitant exclamation doesn't so much evoke women's capacity for adaptation as the psychosomatic flexibility of the maturity a woman attains after having gone beyond the reefs of phallic claims and envy. But it is above all the *specific realization* of these common traits that interested me, in order to invite my readers not to try to be "like," but to seek their own incomparable selves.

The recognition and acknowledgment of male/female parity, often to the detriment of men, has led to a certain crisis of masculine identity, more and more openly. All the same, and over and beyond the war of the sexes that has marked the twentieth century, in the conclusion to these three volumes I assert that another era is opening up. With the psychic bisexuality proper to both sexes, though more affirmed in women, with the more or less monstrous or audacious advances of science in the field of procreation and the impact of these experiments upon the couple and the modern family, it seems to me that each subject invents, for himself, his own particular sex: this is where his genius, which is his creativity, lies.

How long, in fact, will the procreation of the species require a man and a woman? Without going to the extremes of science fiction's apocalyptic or beneficial surprises, we must nonetheless note that subjective creativity—from the beginning and more than ever since the emancipation of the "second sex"—brings into play and causes biological sexual dichotomy. Further, this incommensurable thing that we call genius can only take place through the risks that each person is capable of taking by calling into question his or her way of thinking, language, time, and all identity (sexual, national, ethnic, professional, religious, philosophical, and so forth) that these shelter.

Women, traditionally relegated to reproductive tasks but having acceded to subjective excellence in every domain, highlight the special meaning I give to the idea of genius, by shifting it away from ontotheology and the Romantic philosophy of "great men" and associating it with sharable singularity. With them, more imperiously than with men, taking sexual difference into consideration means including in *genius* the corporal substratum of drives and sensations and envisaging the hypothesis that the process of sublimation is perpetually off balance, at the junction of biology and sense, as I've said.

In this vortex the amorous bond itself becomes more complex, revealing not only its latent delirium but once again its dependency upon our intrinsic animality as well as upon the ecosystem and its potential for creating new symbolic virtuosities or virtualities. Unbelieving as concerns the hypothetical "great men," we do admire the magnificent varieties of strangeness gained from seeming quirkiness or even weakness and celebrate more readily the keyboard genius of Glenn Gould playing Bach or the sensual genius of the "incurably romantic" Marilyn Monroe or the acrobatic genius of the football player Ronaldinho or the discreet genius of this or that geneticist discoverer in his laboratory; at times we reserve the term for the extrahuman, extolling, like Musil, the "genius of a horse," or Colette, the genius of an orchid, "with more allure than a jaguar," "a more potent charm than any other game bird or animal."

Obsolete, genius? To be sure, if you are looking, along with a sad philosopher, for the "will" of a supposed "universal genius." You are right, more than ever we lack "genius." And the depersonalized "one" that we are becoming do ask for more—whenever here and there, modest or incisive singularities awake and take cognizance of the desire to surpass themselves, which, unbeknownst to them, characterizes them in astonishing experiences that surpass them. All the same, our present nihilism is not due to the absence of extraordinary geniuses: the Mozarts and the Michelangelos have always been and remain rare. Nihilistic depression comes from the programmed decline of the singularity that is "intelligence acting through love" which slumbers within each one of us and which, in longing to encounter the totally other, recognizes what is extraordinary in him or in her, makes it exist in the space of time, and takes inspiration from it in order not to die itself of boredom in a world devoid of a beyond.

You have also been interested in the genius of maternity. Maybe because
sublimation is not turned on or off at will, but depends a great deal upon
the first subliminatory bond, that between mother and child?

Yes, today we lack a discourse on maternity. The genius of Christianity has given the world this woman "unique in her sex," as a medieval poem says, the mother of God: the Virgin Mary. I have tried to approach this in "Stabat Mater," my favorite chapter in my book *Tales of Love* (1987). But, beyond the Virgin Mary, what do we know, what do we have to say today about maternal passion? Does what was once a "beyond" not seem to take refuge in the maternal belly today? Omnipotence and madness of mothers: *the desire* for maternity at any cost goes hand in hand with the *denial of pregnancy and the denial of maternity*—up to the crimes of infanticide that are a staple of the news. But it is the key vocation of motherhood I wish to stress: that which consists in rendering it less heatedly passionate so as to transmit language alone, along with the capacity for thought.

Freud was convinced that "loving one's neighbor as oneself" is an illusion, a pious wish of the Gospels. Indeed, such love is only possible for Saint Francis and rare mystics of that ilk. I myself claim that "loving one's neighbor as oneself" returns us to the enigma— darker even than the mystery of gestation—that is the "good enough mother": she who allows the *infans* to create the transitional space permissive of thought.

On the cultural level, I have noted that "feminine genius" (even outside the experience of maternity and in undertakings as diverse as those of Hannah Arendt, Melanie Klein, or Colette) shows the presence of an *object bond* right from the start of psychic life. And this contrary to Freud's postulation of a "narcissism without object" at birth and contrary to "masculine genius" (philosophers, artists) more given to solipsist incantation and to the dramas of subjectivity per se. That said, affirming that for a woman, and even more so for a mother, *there is an other* right from the beginning, is in no sense idyllic. For this precocious object relation is characterized by instability, an instability forever ready to veer toward maniacal exaltation or toward depression and aggression: him or me, projection-identification.

Nonetheless, this drama represents an opportunity, for passion may allow the mother *to elaborate a possible bond with the other:* to elaborate the passionate destructiveness underneath all kinds of bonds that the maternal experience allows us to touch to the quick ("I love him and I hate him"). This is the reason that motherhood, with its violent loves and hates, resembles an *analysis of marginal states and perversions.* I share the opinion of authors as diverse as François Perrier and André Green, for whom feminine sexuality shelters in motherhood in order to live out its perversion and madness, which may also be a chance to work them through. Seductions, making a fetish of the infant body and its accessories, mood swings, maniacal states—it is not unusual that even the possibility of thought is at risk under the influence of such maternal passion. It becomes demoniacal in appearance, conjuring up the fury of ethnic wars, where we know that the most ferocious conflicts are those involving the smallest differences: those one wages against oneself via one's nearest and dearest (as the trials I mentioned, of mothers accused of infanticide, prove).

Still, a certain *detachment-dispassion* occurs in most cases. It is from it that maternal love takes in the end its vital, psychic power to support. Since most mothers are not in analysis, we must admit that something, in the very structure of the experience of motherhood, is favorable to this metabolism of *passion* into a kind of *dispassion.* I suggest we consider three factors within the maternal passion itself: the role of the father, time, and the apprenticeship of language.

I won't go into the father or his representative's essential role, which leads to a reappropriation of the triangular oedipal structure, such that the mother remakes, repairs, or analyses her own Oedipus, which the little girl she was failed, always to some degree, to do. But I'll say a few words about *time* and *language* in the maternal passion.

I cannot overemphasize that the *apprenticeship of language* by the child implies a reapprenticeship of language by the mother. In the projective identification of mother and child, the progenitor inhabits the mouth, the lungs, the digestive tube of her offspring and, in accompanying the echolalia, guides them toward signs, phrases, tales: *infans* becomes infant, a speaking subject. As this takes place, each mother accomplishes in her own way her Proustian search for "lost time": it is in speaking the language of her child that a woman, step by step, remedies the *noncongruence* (as cognitists say), the abyss between affect and cognition, of which the hysteric endlessly complains.

As for time, which, in Western philosophy always refers to the time of *death,* which also of course haunts the experience of motherhood, the mother's experience of time is marked by another kind of caesura: that of the *beginning.* Of course, both parents are aware that conception and childbirth are the principle, initiating acts; but the mother feels this even more strongly because her own body is implicated. For her, birth's new beginning is not only a conjuration of death. Philosophers teach us that freedom's logic does not reside in a transgression, as one might easily think, but in the capacity to begin. Winnicott himself suggested that the baby's exit from the womb toward birth only takes place when it is sufficiently free in its movements, when it reaches a certain level of biopsychological completion, a certain autonomy: beginning and autonomy, for this psychoanalyst, might well be two aspects of the same state. *The time* of the mother is confronted with this opening, with this beginning— or with beginnings, in the plural, when she brings several children into the world or when she becomes a grandmother with her grandchildren. The ephemerality of the life we give doubtless brings with it worries and anxieties, but these are covered up by a feeling of wonderment before the ephemeral seen as a rebeginning. I call the maternal experience of temporality, which is neither the instant nor the inexorable passage of time (which preoccupies men, more easily obsessive than women), a *duration with new beginnings.* Freedom means having the courage to start over: such is the philosophy of maternity.

Thus I arrive at the maternal passion's capacity for sublimation. *Because it is a continuous sublimation, maternal passion makes the child's creativity possible.* The acquisition of language and thought by the child depend upon the paternal function as well as upon maternal support. How could this happen if women themselves were incapable of sublimation, as Freud insinuated? The founder of psychoanalysis advanced this excommunication recklessly, perhaps having in mind hysterical excitability, refractory to symbolization. On the other hand, and unlike the hysteria of which it is not unaware, maternal passion enacts a transformation of the libido such that sexualization is postponed by tenderness, whereas narcissistic exaltation, with its melancholic underside, all the way to "maternal madness," with its lasting grip, yields to a *subliminatory cycle* in which the mother constitutes herself in differentiating herself from the newborn.

Freud observed just such a subliminatory cycle in the emission and reception of the *witticism*. In effect, the author of the witticism neutralizes his affects by communicating only his apparent thought: he stands back from his drives and his latent thought; he is invested only in his hearer's reaction; finally the pleasure of the raconteur increases when his hearer catches the hidden sense of the witticism, even if it's a trap! This subliminatory cycle resembles what happens during the exchange of signifiers between mother and child: emission of "enigmatic signifiers," verbal or preverbal; the mother stands back from her drives, attending to the child's reactions; a "bonus" or extra encouragement given to the child's response: she is not invested in her own message, only in the response; at the end of this cycle the mother obtains an even greater pleasure from the child's response, which she extols and encourages.

As you see, this subliminatory cycle is not without subliminatory perversity in the mother's behavior and speech: since the mother defers her immediate hold over the child, the better to obtain pleasure from its development or, more exactly from her role as the holder of meaning, which the child must nevertheless grasp in order for there to be a "witticism"! Sacred mother! Thus she detaches herself from her own ambivalent passion and allows the child to create a proper language, a language of its own: which is the equivalent of choosing a language foreign to that of the mother or even a foreign language, period.

Those who claim that the maternal passion is humorless are mistaken: if mothers can transform their hold over their child into a subliminatory cycle resembling that of a witticism, and thereby encourage the pleasure of thought, they support Hegel's contention that women are "the eternal irony of the community."

In the end, it is through a progressive dispassion and/or by her aptitude for sublimation that the mother lets the child interiorize and represent *not the* mother ("nothing can represent the maternal object," writes André Green), but *the absence of the* mother: if and only if she gives the child the freedom to appropriate maternal thought, recreating this in its own way of thinking-representing. The "good enough mother" might be the one who can go away, making a place for the child to have *the pleasure* of *thinking her.*

A sort of *symbolic matricide* thus occurs, with the acquisition of language and of thought by the child who no longer has—or who has less—the need to revel in the mother's body than in the pleasure of thought, first of all with her, next for himself, in place of her. Providing the mother is able to make her message not a domineering kind of inveiglement, but a witticism. Only if the dispassion is underway in the maternal passion does the sublimation carry over from the *body to thinking* and ground thereby the development of the child's thought. Maternal passion is not a kind of witchcraft, since it is capable of transforming itself into a witticism. And of transmitting, along with the DNA, the keys to culture.

As you can see, maternal passion appeared to us *split* between holding and sublimation. Because of this split, mothers are in constant danger of going mad; it also offers them the chance of culture. Religious myths wove their webs around this split. Woman is both a "hole" (this is the meaning of the word *woman* in Hebrew: *nekeva*) and a queen in the Bible; the Virgin is a "hole" in the Christian trinity father/son/holy spirit *and* queen of the church. Through such constructions of the imagination, religions would address the maternal split: acknowledging it, they perpetuated it, provided a kind of equilibrium. A sort of working through of maternal madness came about nonetheless, making possible the existence of a humanity endowed with a complex psychic apparatus, capable of both an inner life and creativity in the outer world.

On the other hand, from aiming all our projectors at biological and social life, but also at sexual freedom and equality, we find ourselves the first civilization *without a discourse on the complexity of the vocation of motherhood.* I dream of helping to remedy this in order to encourage mothers and those who assist them (gynecologists, obstetricians, midwives, psychologists, analysts) and to refine our knowledge of this passion, pregnant with madness and sublimity. Mothers today are in need of such a discourse.

Only relatively recently has genius been declined in the feminine, allowing it to manifest itself fully and gain recognition in our culture. Still, there is one aspect—which indeed concerns religiosity—sainthood, mysticism, where the discourse on feminine genius may find its most telling forebears. You yourself have tried to plumb this theme through your studies of a figure such as Saint Teresa of Avila. If it is true that genius, the singularity, involves tremendous suffering, can one say that sainthood, mysticism, the ecstasy of Saint Teresa of Avila interest you precisely as a kind of alchemy of suffering? What is the passion according to Teresa of Avila?

I am indeed absorbed in the writing of a book, a mixture of novel and essay, about Teresa of Avila, which I am not sure will ever be published.[2] As you know, Teresa of Avila (1515–1582) lived and wrote about an extravagant experience, which we call mystical, at a time when, in Spain, the power and the glory of the Conquistadors and the Golden Age had begun their decline. In addition, Erasmus and Luther had upset traditional beliefs: new Catholics such as the Alumbrados were attracting Jews and women; the Inquisition put all the books written in Castilian on the Index, and trials attesting to *limpieza de sangre* were increasingly frequent. Daughter of a *cristiana vieja* and a *converso,* Teresa in her childhood witnessed the trial against her paternal family, which was obliged to prove that it was indeed Christian, not Jewish. Her practice, as a nun, of spiritual concentration, that is, the mental prayer of amorous fusion with God that was to lead to her ecstasies, was brought before the Inquisition. Then the Counter-Reformation discovered the extraordinary complexity of her experience, and her usefulness to a Church that was trying to wed asceticism (as the Protestants demanded) to the intensity of the supernatural (good for popular faith). Teresa de Ahumada y Cepeda was beatified in 1614 (thirty-two years after her death), canonized in 1622 (forty years after her death), and in 1970, following Vatican II, became, along with Catherine of Sienna, the first female Doctor of the Church.

A SAINT OF THE COUNTER-REFORMATION

How to sum up the nearly one thousand pages amassed on my computer in which I try to encounter her? Forgive me this simplification. Catholic mysticism (with its two peaks: Rhenan mysticism in the twelfth century and then, after the Council of Trent and the Counter-Reformation, above all, the Spaniards Teresa of Avila and her friend John of the Cross) was in a place of *internal exclusion* from Catholicism: a margin revelatory of its heart. Teresa's writing arises from this paradoxical position as well as her founding work as a Discalced or Barefoot Carmelite. I am particularly attached to three aspects of the thought this woman brought to a paroxysm and clarity never previously attained.

Christian Faith rests upon an indelible confidence in the existence of an Ideal Father, and upon absolute love for this loving Father, who is seen, quite simply, as the foundation of the speaking
subject, who is, consequently, none other than the subject of loving
speech. The Father of Agape or Amor, therefore, not Eros, although
these two kinds of love come together, when they are not opposed,
in Christian histories. "I love because I am loved, therefore I am,"
could be the believer's syllogism, which Teresa enacts in her visions
and ecstasies. This syllogism takes us back to the "loving father of
individual prehistory," whom we encountered with Freud at the start
of our discussion. Obviously, the first reference of Teresa, and other
mystics, is the sublime Song of Songs: a meshing of eroticism and
sublimation, of presence and flight, of body and words.

However, this extreme idealization is only maintained in its
unadulterated state along with an injunction to repression, in the
exoteric message of the Church. The mystic, on the other hand, in
his internal exclusion, does not stop sexualizing the amorous idealization, even if the idealizing remains essential. Freud has shown
the logic of these alternations in the economy of the drives ("Drives
and Their Destinies"): when processes and excitations exceed certain quantitative limits, they are eroticized. Mystics, and Teresa
above all, not only take part in this reversal, but some of them, and
Teresa more than others, are able to name them. From that point on-
ward, the alternation idealization-desexualization-resexualization
and vice versa transforms the love for the Ideal Father into an un-
stoppable impulsive violence, into a *passion for the Father which is in truth
a sadomasochistic père-version* [turning toward the father]. Severe fasting,
penitence, flagellations—including with nettles on the wounds—
convulsions, all the way to epileptic comas that take advantage of
the mystic's neuronal or hormonal frailties: these are only a few
of the extravagances that mark these "exiles of the self" in Him (to
use an expression of Teresa's), the transferences in the Other (to use

my language). Are these experiences rooted in the phantasm of the "beaten child" that Freud discovered in his patients' unconscious? Not exactly. More than the "beaten child," it is the tortured Son-Father or (to stick with Freud) the "beaten Father" that Christianity venerates in the Passion of Christ, whom the believer identifies with, as does, in a paroxysmal manner, the orant, or praying figure, at his prayers. A gratifying way if ever there was one to support suffering humanity, but the submissive femininity of both sexes as well, all the way to unbearable manifestations of violence. Dostoyevsky's comment: "It is too idealistic and because of this cruel" (*The Humiliated and Offended*) may be read as a summary of the mystic's—and Teresa's—père-version.

However, this incitement to suffering is relieved by oral satisfaction: the Eucharist reconciles the believer with the Son-Father tortured to death and, to an even greater extent, gives the body of this suffering Man, which "I" myself become when I swallow the Other, the attributes of a good and nurturing mother. Numerous melancholics and anorexics of the Middle Ages betook themselves to the churches to eat a single kind of food: a flake of the bloody and maltreated body of the God Man. Which allowed them to live for many a year, despite hunger, in the midst of this frenzy, through the sole trickery of an oral satisfaction exalted by a symbolic union. For, from having *oralized the idealization-resexualization*, Christianity also made the *word* itself the ultimate object of desire and love: "It is not what goes into the mouth that defiles a man but what comes out of the mouth that defiles . . . " (Matthew 15:11 and Mark 7:15). As a consequence of this, and in the phantasm, genitality is abolished by being displaced onto the pleasure of being reborn through this orality, closely supervised so as to attain absolute purification. "Holy anorexia" (Rudolph M. Bell) is the result.

The rebirth at stake is doubly assured: by the cannibalistic identification with the Son-Father beaten to death and by the reconquest of Time in a species of eternity of the word. This latter then becomes the principle object of desire (object *a*), by the grace of a narration open to the infinite quest of sense, necessarily subjective. For Teresa, the preferred experiences of this work are of necessity *writing* (as elucidation of the experience) and *foundation* (a political act that renovates Carmelite institutional space and temporality).

Teresa undertook to reform the "shoed" Carmelites into "barefoot" Carmelites some time after having begun writing *The Book of Her Life* (1560), and she continued writing while founding seventeen monasteries in twenty years. She proves herself, in so doing, to be both "the most virile of the monks"—"I am not a woman, I have a hard heart" (she writes)—and a convinced defender of feminine specificity: in affirming, for example, that women are more apt than men to practice the spiritual discipline of prayer, by standing up to the hierarchy of the Church, or by making use of the monarchy to help her develop feminine monasticism.

"WRITE THIS FICTION SO PEOPLE CAN UNDERSTAND"

Shall I close with a few aspects of her visions and her writing?

The only girl in a family of seven boys (until the birth of two little latecomers, a girl and boy), very attached to her mother and father, to her brother Rodrigo, to her paternal uncle Pedro, and to her cousin the son of Francisco, her other paternal uncle, in a family with incestuous overtones that, though comfortably off, was growing poorer, Teresa lost her mother at the age of thirteen. When she decided to become a Carmelite and took the habit in the Convent of the Incarnation on November 2, 1536, she was twenty-one years old, and her body was a battlefield: between the *guilty desires* that she only hints at in her *Life*, saying that her confessors forbade her to enlarge on them, and the *idealizing exaltation* as seen in her intense cult for Mary (the virgin mother) and Joseph (the symbolic father). In her autobiography, with peerless lucidity, she confides that her torments led to convulsions and losses of consciousness, sometimes followed by comas of up to four days: after the Spaniard E. Garcia-Albea, Dr Pierre Vercelletto, the French epilepsy specialist, was to diagnose a "temporal epilepsy."

These crises, however, went hand in hand with the extraordinary "visions" the nun described as auras: not "views" by the "eyes of the body," but what I would be tempted to call incarnate phantasms; that is, perceptions by all the senses together, of the enveloping, reassuring, loving presence of the Spouse. The ideal, and therefore cruel Father, who persecuted her by hurting her right to the bone, is transformed into a loving Father: Theresa was successful where President Schreber (recall how in 1911 Freud interpreted the testimony of this magistrate who thought himself persecuted by a fierce and divine father) failed: God no longer judged her, or at any rate less and less, because He loved her.

The sequencing of some of the "visions" Teresa was to reconstruct in her *Life* conveys the logic of this saving alchemy. To begin with, the "vision"—an "image" that is not received by the eyes of the body—brings her into the presence of a "stern face" that disapproves of the young nun's overly casual "visitors." Next the "vision" becomes a "toad" that grows and grows: a hallucination of the sexual organ of the visitor? Finally, the suffering Man himself appears in the form of a statue of Christ Teresa had seen in the monastery courtyard: a martyred man whose suffering she is ravished to identify with, to expiate her torments.

Ravished is the word: at last Teresa is united with "Christ as man" (*Cristo como hombre*); she appropriates him—"certain that the Lord was within me" (*dentro de mí*). "After that I could not for an instant doubt that he was in me or that I myself was engulfed in him" (*yo todo engolfada en él*) (Life 10:1). At the height of her exaltation all her senses suddenly veer toward utter nothingness: the soul is deprived of all capacity for "work," nothing but "abandon," exquisite, blissful passivity: "deprived even of sentiment" (18:4), "a sort of delirium" (18:13);

"one feels nothing, one yields to the bliss without knowing what bliss it is" (18:1). Positive and negative, joy and extreme pain, together or in alternation. This brew of plentitude and sensory emptying crushes the body and exiles it in a syncope where the psyche is in its turn annihilated, beyond the self, until the soul becomes capable of taking up the tale of this state of "loss." The narration that ensues was recounted first to her Dominican and Jesuit confessors, who were troubled or seduced, and then they allowed and finally urged her to write it down. The high point of these "visions" with their fiery sensuality is to be found in the masterly description of her *Transfixion*, which Bernini reconstructed in marble (1646) and so delighted Lacan in his seminar *Encore* (1972–73).

As you can see, the enigma of Teresa lies, to my mind, less in her ravishments than in the tales she tells of them: let's see, do the ravishments exist outside her tales? Epilepsy or no epilepsy, it is the screen of the epileptic shock, the impulse discharge, as filtered through the Catholic code, *in Teresa's Castilian language,* that assured her biological survival and guaranteed, as well, that her experience would live on in cultural memory. The writer was perfectly aware of this: "make this fiction (*hacer esta ficción*) so that people may understand," she writes in *The Way of Perfection* (28:10).

As far as Teresa's "fiction" goes, I would first keep in mind this state that her religion describes as ecstatic and that I would qualify as *regression* or even what Winnicott calls a *psychosoma:* another version of the "oceanic feeling." Indeed, it is by means of a fiction involving water—Teresa's readers will be familiar with her variations on the "four waters" in which she is bathed—that the nun describes her immersion in the Other and her sense of losing the boundaries of the self. More than a metaphor, water for Teresa is a veritable metamorphosis into the pain-and-joy of becoming fluid, of liquefying oneself *to be other.* Finally, she finds her identification with the divine at the heart of her *Interior Castle* in the seventh mansion: and it is not the least paradoxical aspect of this God according to Teresa, not to be located save in the depths . . . of the soul of this woman writer.

Husserl wrote that "'fiction' is the vital element in phenomenology as in all the eidetic sciences." We may understand by this that fiction "fertilizes" abstraction by using rich and precise sensorial data transposed into clear images. Never perhaps has this value of fiction as "vital element" for the knowledge of "eternal truths" been quite so justified as in Teresa's use of water to convey in writing her states of prayer. A "telling" example of the quest of sublimation through speech aspiring to merge with the other in the experience of amorous regression-exaltation.

Confessors and editors were to tone down this exorbitant claim, which for a period attracted the attention of the Inquisition itself until, following the Council of Trent, the writer's saintliness was recognized.

But this had its consequences.

The first of these would be Teresa's indomitable irony, not all that surprising given that she seems to have been a fine chess player. On a sheet of paper that didn't make it into *The Way of Perfection*, Teresa advises her sisters to play chess in the monasteries, even against the rules, in order to "checkmate the Lord"! An impertinence that resonates with the famous formula of Meister Eckhart: "I ask God to leave me free me of God."

The second was formulated by Leibniz. On December 10, 1696, in a letter to Morell, he wrote: "As far as Saint Teresa goes, you are right to admire her works; I found there the lovely thought that the soul must conceive of things as if there was only it and God in the world. Which gives rise to considerable philosophical thought, which I've found useful for one of my hypotheses." Teresa the inspirer of Leibniz's infinity-containing monads? Teresa the precursor of infinitesimal calculus?

The other side of this subliminatory passion: sublime in its risks, sublime in its pleasures, and sublimely lucid—is of course the amount of suffering imposed and endured, which modernists insult as *sadomasochism*. The modernists that we are claim to have done with that. Are we so sure? And at what cost?

Let's return to the question of the continuity and discontinuity of European culture. In your books, notably in Tales of Love, *you have reflected a great deal upon the impact of Greek culture, and of Judaism and Christianity, recalling as well the central role played by the Protestant Reformation, the Council of Trent, and of course the Enlightenment on what we call "modernity." But before harking back to this heritage, let's consider this: Sectarianism today spares no religion. However, can one consider that the three monotheisms do not share the same ontological need to believe? Is not the need to believe different in Judaism, in Christianity, in Islam?*

I have just returned from a marvelous trip to Athens, where I was dazzled, yet again, by the Greek miracle. How not to be when one "climbs" to the Acropolis, when the vestiges, increasingly well restored—but that will always lack a roof—shelter us in the splendor of their architecture, whose geometrical soundness vies with the elegance of the Caryatids. These women, several centuries old, who not only were not veiled but excelled at singing and dance . . . A humanity open to the cosmos that thinks about being even as it relishes sensual pleasure, that takes pleasure in being while thinking. Today, the vanished roofs of the ancient temples accentuate this existential and philosophical truth and make it immediately, delightfully perceptible . . . And look, down below the first Byzantine domes enclose the open space! Space curves around itself, it cuts man off from the world. But Judeo-Christianity does not do away with vastness of Greek being. It bends it inward, it hollows out "inwardness," never ceasing to link it to the Great Other, right to the unnameable, which must be named again and again, because in the beginning was the Word, which is Love, and Logos prides itself on embracing love up until the point of death itself . . . Christianity's genius and its nightmares . . . We can barely evoke even the rudiments of this debate in this no-holds-barred overview that you have proposed today.

At the risk of contradicting you, I must say I haven't "reflected a great deal" upon the relationship between Greek culture and Christianity, nor upon the relationship between the three monotheisms. Or not enough, such a task is beyond me, I only stutter at it, remembering my father, so well-versed in Orthodox theology. I am indebted to Philippe Sollers in the domain of Catholicism, this is something we discuss all the time, and I've also benefited from the knowledge of a few rare believer-friends, Catholic or Jewish. But, to be frank, in my work as a psychoanalyst, as a literary theorist, as a writer, I hardly ever come up against your questions, notably as concerns contemporary developments in psychoanalysis, which, in affirming its knowledge of psychic life, encourages exploration of marginal states, but also of those enigmatic regions that religious experiences still are. A psychoanalytic meeting in New York on the topic of the "dead Father," an important figure in the history of religions as well as a genuine clinical experience, recently led me to some reflections that might perhaps sketch an answer to your question: by rereading Freud's *Totem and Taboo* (1912) together with "A Child Is Being Beaten" (1919) in light of my clinical knowledge of the "desire for the father," sadomasochism and its sublimation.

What does Freud say? Societies are founded on the *incest prohibition* (he returns to this in "A Child Is Being Beaten"—transgressing this prohibition leads to guilt and punishment) and on the *murder of the father* (which he analyzes from *Totem and Taboo* up to and including *Moses and Monotheism*). Religions constantly return to these two events, which they reinforce or elucidate in their own way: by accumulating illusions even as they reveal unconscious truths. Reinforcing social codes, but often asocial or even antisocial, religions may harden into obscurantism, just as they may be received as a revelation, in the strongest sense of the term, of the unconscious logic imposed by, unless it transgresses, the *prohibition against incest* and *murdering the father*. However partial this revelation may be, however illusory or dogmatic its promises and consolations, precisely because it offers interpretations affecting the basis of the social pact, it gives breathing space to social constraints. It seduces *homo oeconomicus* and *homo politicus,* doubled from time immemorial by *homo religiosis.*

Let me go back to the "desire for the father" and the "murder of the father." We remember that, for Freud, the murder of the father is a *historical reality* in human civilization. Similarly, in Christianity, Jesus Christ is a historical person, and the murder believers commemorate is a real murder. I take these considerations into account while setting myself apart from them in what follows. I am only interested in the *psychic reality* that these events generate in believer subjects, in the representations or the phantasms, leaving aside the question whether these events really happened or not. Furthermore, although Christ is the *Son,* according to the Gospels, I shall take into consideration the logic according to which it is also the *Father* (God himself) who is put to death in the passion (Saint Paul already reminded us of this, before Hegel and Nietzsche). Indeed, in the logic of the Trinity, it seems difficult to dissociate the suffering to death of the son from that of the father who is consubstantial with him.

Besides, the common fantasy that "a child is being beaten" (generally a boy, in the unconscious of both the girl and the boy), abreacts according to the founder of psychoanalysis the infantile guilt provoked by incestuous desire toward the father and by the incest prohibition that imposes the father's law as the basis of the social bond.

Question: what happens if Jesus is not only a beaten child or a brother but a beaten father—and beaten to death?

In mixing up the son (the beaten boy) *and* the father (authority figure), this scenario has the advantage of *both* relieving the incestuous guilt that weighs upon the *desire* for the sovereign Father, that

Other, and encouraging virile *identification* (including in the case of the girl or woman) with this *tortured* man: a glorious identification, gratifying, but in the guise of a masochism that this double impulse enhances the value of, even recommends. "This beaten father and/or brother is my double, my fellow, my alter ego (says the man of faith), he is me with a male organ (adds the woman)."

The passion of the father,
my fellow, my brother

So the way is clear in the unconscious for the father as *agent of the Law and of the Forbidden* to amalgamate with "I": beloved son or daughter of that father and *subject of the guilty love passion*. Father the superman is humanized; even more, he is feminized by his suffering, and it is precisely in this that he becomes for me both a double (replica of my weakness, guilt, mortality . . .) and an ideal (I am united with him in the promise of eternity, of salvation). A complicit "we" results from this by and in the passion of the father, henceforth we share love along with the guilt and punishment. "We are both of us in love and, guilty, we ought to be beaten to death together, death initiates our reunion in the beyond": such might be the believer's motto.

It follows that, for the unconscious, these father/son and father/daughter reunions *put the incest prohibition on hold* in and through the suffering of the two loving-and-punished protagonists, so that their common *suffering* is necessarily experienced as a *wedding*. The sexualized pain, under "the whip of faith," in the identification with the beaten-to-death father, becomes the paradise of masochism. And there will be no other outcome than its own staging-in-signs: words—phrases—tales; sound; images . . . the Infinite of representations and cultures.

At this point, we can see that in putting *the phantasm of the tortured-to-death son-father,* which calls out to the identification of humans, at the climax of the Gospel story Christianity does not just reinforce the prohibitions, as it is generally accused of doing. But, paradoxically, as it assumes them, it *displaces* them and clears the way for their perlaboration or sublimation.

In being beaten in his phantasms or actings out *as* this Son-Father, the subject can tear out, liberate his unconscious desires for the guilty suffering that goes along with them, and settle into what it is necessary to call a sovereign, divine suffering. Not the suffering of guilt, or *transgression,* but suffering as the sole path to *union* with the ideal of the Father. A new kind of suffering: Christlike or Christian, which is not the other side of the Law, but a suspension of the Law and of guilt, in favor of, to be precise, an *orgasmic pleasure [jouissance] in idealized suffering.* Pleasure of the call, of languishing, of the essential unquenched nature of desire for the father: the suffering-delight in the ambivalence of the père-version. The Son-Father cavalry neither renders suffering banal nor permits incest. But, through its glory and thanks to our desire for the father, with the father, this suffering-together, this compassion, is about to avow and justify incest along with the excruciating pain of this sin. Far beyond pleasure [*plaisir*], what is at stake here is bliss [*jouir*] in the sense in which "bliss" [*jouir*] with the Son-Father is a bliss [*jouir*] to death, and the Christlike scenario awakens this unconscious truth. Nietzsche says it emphatically: "that which, for two millenaries, calls itself Christian, rests upon a psychological misunderstanding of oneself. . . . When we examine that which calls itself Christian more closely, what predominates, all its faith notwithstanding, are the instincts, and what instincts!" (*The Antichrist*). Yes, but also what superb storytelling, hence a kind of understanding, of this misunderstanding and of the instincts themselves! Why?

Because the adoration of the tortured or beaten-to-death Son-Father has, along with its invitation to pleasure, another consequence, even more fundamental: with and beyond the surreptitiously accepted *incestuous link* with the Son-Father is the *symbolic activity* itself, which the believer is invited to eroticize via the paternal passion, to develop, to glorify, to love for itself. How?

PLEASURES OF FLESH-PLEASURES OF REPRESENTATION

The activity of representing-speaking-thinking, attributed to the father in patrilineal societies, which links me to him, becomes—in the
Christly scheme of things—the special domain of the bliss [*jouissance*]
that embraces and goes beyond sadomasochistic pleasure: this is what
offers itself after all as a "realm" in which suffering is deployed, justified, appeased—and rekindled. With Freud, *sublimation* is the name
given to this displacement of the pleasure, from the body and the
sexual organs, into representation. *Père-version and sublimation can hence
be seen as the two sides of this softening, or even this fabulous suspension of the incest
prohibition, which the Son-Father, beaten in my place, brings about.*

No other religion, even that of the Greek gods, encouraged the
experience of sublimation quite so effectively as the Son-Father
beaten to death. By means of this phantasm, Christianity maintains
on the one hand the inaccessible ideal (Jesus is an extrasensible God,
a forbidden Father who forbids me to touch, perceive, or smell him),
on the other hand, without any fear of contradiction, the Christian
faith also resexualizes the ideal Son-Father whose happy suffering
associates me, through my guilt, with the passion, by means of the
Eucharist initially, with the intense activity of representation that
culminates in the aesthetic venture.

Whatever may have been the former excesses and the modern
versions of these, let us try to hold onto the intrapsychic truth of this
belief, which I would sum up as follows: the myth of the beaten-to-
death Son-Father says the *incest prohibition is not just a loss of pleasure;* it
also invites the excitement to take a *leap on the spot* and, while staying
with me, to transit through my sensory and genital organs and fasten
itself to a *psychic representation* and to psychic acts: ideality, symbolism,
thought, art.

Great artists (Mozart, Picasso) feel this intense phantasmic dia-
lect during creation's sustained fever. Catholicism, particularly with
and after the rupture of the Baroque, brilliantly favored it by putting

into signs this happy culpability that constantly transgresses—even as it maintains them—the sexual or carnal prohibitions.

A TRAVERSING OF THE DEATH INSTINCT?

But the "A Son-Father is beaten to death" phantasm is not content, strictly speaking, to *liberate* the death instinct as *sadomasochistic aggressiveness* and to bring it to its paroxysm in a kind of orgasmic pleasure [*jouissance*]. In addition, it confronts this drive in its radically Freudian sense: it takes the death instinct right to the *undoing* [*déliaison*] (A. Green) of the bonds of the drives and of life itself. This is exactly what is implied in the Gospel story when God the Father himself returns to the nothingness. Is not the *kénose* or Christly "annulment" in the descent into hell not the death of God himself? From this ensues, very quickly, the reconciliation of the Son with the Father by means of the resurrection. While being a denial of death, the theme of the resurrection is received by the believer as an invitation to follow body and soul the desire for the Son-Father: an invitation to recall every station of the way, to live and to sublimate them. Marvels of Christian experience and art!

Freud saw that the incest prohibition upon which human culture rests begins with the discovery, by the brothers, that the father is an animal to kill. *Totem*—we keep only the *Taboo* so as to transform it into a set of rules for the exchange of women, into laws, into names, into language, into sense.

Christianity not only allowed the putting to death of the Son-Father, but associated this murder with the desire for the Father, a desire that cannot be separated from the guilt to which the transgression of the incest prohibition gives rise; the two impulses together fan the flames of ek-static pleasure. Such is *the particular solution* that Christianity has managed to impose upon the authority of the universal dead father whose religious commemoration characterizes the human condition. From this, Christianity, and Catholicism, especially after the

Counter-Reformation, brought about a deep mutation in the universal need to believe. It absorbed the Greco-Roman body: it reabsorbed the antique body rediscovered by the humanists, pushing it to its limits in an unbridled representation of the Passion of Man. Painting, music, literature, caught up in this, had to develop the perceptions-sensations of men and women, as explored by mysticism, glorified by Baroque art. And radically change the subject of monotheism.

This exuberance carries along with it an exquisite knowledge of the passions whose deadly explosion it cannot restrain, when the need to believe—and to take pleasure in [*jouir*]—wins out over the desire for knowledge and justice. The banalizing of evil, the horror of totalitarianism's declaring "the superfluity of human life," remain enigmatic still as far as both the need to believe and economic, sociological, political rationality are concerned. The Freudian discovery and its developments alone insist upon the sadomasochistic desire for the law of the father, which ever and always nourishes moral order, and upon the black Eros that underpins the père-version and the sublimation of this *homo religiosis* that *homo sapiens* is.

The beginning of the third millennium, with the collapse of paternal and political authority and the massive return of the *need to believe* gives us a glimpse of something more: the dead father, who conditions the existence of *homo religiosis,* died on the cross two thousand years ago, but the promise of his resurrection is not to be sought either in the beyond or in the vile world. Where, then?

The founder of psychoanalysis began by putting love on his couch. So as to go back to the love of the father and the mother, and in betting (which is not the domain of faith, but rather that of gambling) that "I" can set myself free from my genitors, maybe even from myself and my loves, on the condition that I am in analysis, in the perpetual dissolution of the transference-countertransference. Which supposes that there is not only *one* Father loved and beaten to death, but *many* paternal and many beloved figures, in which I take pleasure [*jouir*], whom I assassinate and resurrect whenever I speak, love, and think. Addressing psychoanalysts interested in modern variants of the "dead Father" or the "murder of the Father," I have maintained that the need to believe is a group of père-versions that the speaking being cannot get rid of; that the mère-versions themselves, encouraged by feminism, the pill, and different sorts of assisted conception, are part of this; that the "shock of religions" can be clarified if not elucidated by our listening. No doubt this is why the opening of a permanent forum on these questions has been offered me. Why not in . . . Jerusalem? Clinicians in dialogue with religious specialists and theologians. What if this were the eternal return of Freud?

INFINITE ARE THE METAMORPHOSES OF THE DEAD FATHER . . .

We thought "Big Mother" had taken the place of the oedipal Father. The reality is that the Freudian analyst, man or woman, works with a new version of the "paternal function." Neither totemic animal, nor Laius/Oedipus, neither Abraham/Isaac, nor Jesus and his father, forsaking and resuscitating. In the love-hate of the transference, the father is not only loved and hated, or put to death and resurrected, as the Holy Writ would have it; he is literally *atomized,* all the while being reincorporated by the analysand thanks to the experience of transference-countertransference. And this ongoing dissolution-reconstruction, of which the analyst is the guarantor, makes possible the analysis of drug addictions, somatizations, criminal behavior, borderline cases. The subject of the new diseases of the soul comes out of this with a paradoxical identity, which reminds me of the Brownian motion of those Pollock drip paintings called *One.* Where did One go? Am I still One when I analyze or when I am analysand? Yes, but equipped with an undecidable identity, without fixed center or mortiferous repetition; serial music rather, a dance improvised and yet supported by an underlying, open order. Free associations, yes, alluding to a long history that never stops coming back, catching up with us.

Such is the disturbing and fascinating secret of European culture, of European humanity in all its diversity, two thousand years in the grips of Christianity and, for two centuries, in those of its rebellious offshoots, like the Enlightenment. Can psychoanalysis today propose an interpretation of its ever-present hold, and that of the other religions? It will in this way help to clear a space in which elucidation may replace *destructive confrontations* where regression and the explosion of the death instinct face off, the present danger to global humanity.

"Love" having been thus understood and historically situated, we can come back to the unspoken part of your question, which was put to me directly by some friends of Studio Art Mapagne in Tel Aviv: *will the believers of the three monotheisms one day be able to love one another in peace?* You must understand that I am not asking this question in the spirit of someone who *believes* in Love: this latter being an avatar of the drive that, in the human being, is subject to the incest prohibition and to the murder of the father—we can't say this often enough—its violence and its limitations do not make it a remedy. The prophet Jeremiah was aware of this when he proclaimed: "Peace, peace, when there is no peace!" (Jeremiah 8:11). I, for my part, attempt to interpret the meaning of the demand for love, the lack of love and the hope of love, as well as the hate that is the inseparable other side of this: to respond to them with the bonds of friendship and fellow feeling that are apt to ease the passion as well as the compassion—for these are burdened by the offense of which they bear the stigmata, ready to be engulfed in vengeance.

Does Islam share in this trend of monotheism? Where does its warlike spirit come from? Might Allah be closer to the God of Aristotle than God the Creator?

Benedict XVI's recent speech in Ratisbonne revived the question of "reason" according to Islam and also the place it gives to its conception of "holy war." We have seen how the taking of shortcuts can aggravate misunderstandings: I shall try not to add new ones, despite the inevitable holes in this all-too-simplified overview.

You are correct, many specialist speak of the "resemblances" between Allah and the God of Aristotle whom we know is defined as the "Prime Unmoved Mover," on the edge of the universe (*Physics* 8.10), or even as a cause of the world very distant from the world: some would place him at "the source" of Islamic radicalization, right to robotlike obedience and terror! Others, however, remind us that Hellenism and particularly Aristotelianism attracted Islam, but was also a foil for it; that there was a "rationalist" school in the eighth century, which tried to justify faith by reason; that we owe to such great masters as Avicenna and Averroes the "discovery" and diffusion of Aristotle, above all in Christian culture. How venture into this vast domain without knowing the language and lacking all but secondhand information?

Let us remember, at least, that the Aristotelian divine is much more complex than people would have it. Already, in the *Metaphysics*, this prime mover moves the sublunary world like a desirable "love object" (λ, 7); it is capable of "moving without being moved" and is conceived in psychological terms as a "touching" that "touches," in the sense of "moves," without being touched or moved; a transcendence, in short, the world can nonetheless "imitate." In the *Poetics*, however, Aristotle posits a divinity that does not harden into unapproachable theocracy, but engenders a tragic humanism; the wisdom of limits. We are very far, as we see, from the omnipotence of the Islamic legislator who exacts obedience . . . Furthermore, and although this kindly God of the *Metaphysics* in no way resembles the loving God of the Christians, Christian theology was to integrate him into the understanding of the living and loving God (in particular through the rediscovery of Aristotle and Saint Thomas's rereading of him). A "communication of being" was to be established between the Creator and the "substances" of the universe, thus conferring upon him an ontological density. A long history of the interpretation of the Bible and the Gospels in the light of Aristotle's philosophy came out of this, shaping Christian theology, and then Christian and post-Christian philosophy.

WHAT ABOUT THE ROLE OF THE FATHER?

I myself think that, as far as Islam goes, rather than question the influence of Aristotle, we should look into the relation of the divine to the *role of the father*. The pivotal figure of this fatherhood, both juridical and loving, is none other than the biblical Abraham, who spares Isaac: for God is so moved by his obedience to the divine commandment that he suspends, stops, not only the sacrifice of the son but also passion between men, their "oedipal" desire to death (let us say, along with Freud). The way for the messianism of the *pistis* is henceforth open: Jesus and the "faith working through love" of the biblical God (Galatians 5:6) accomplish the destiny of Abraham, since Jesus dies on the cross only to resurrect by and for the love of the Father.

Furthermore, in the long and meticulous development of *Moses and Monotheism* (1939), Freud posits that the murder of Moses, an "eminent father substitute," by his people was the factor that "made Akhenaton take monotheism seriously" and transformed Egyptian monotheism, mirror of the monolithic power of the Pharaoh, into the high spirituality of Mosaic monotheism.

In Islam, the foundational event of the father's murder is presented differently. Freud supposes, still in *Moses and Monotheism,* that in the Mohammedan religion there is a "restoration (*Wiedergewinnung*) of the one, great Original Father (*Urvater*)," but suggests that he "lacks the deepening produced, in the case of Judaism, by the murder perpetrated against the religion's founding figure," a murder that Christianity is, on the other hand, ready to admit. I share this point of view, and I have given you some elements of my reflections upon the place of the tortured and beloved Father-Son in Christianity.

Add to this the fact that there is still some uncertainty, in Islam, as to the person of the son to be sacrificed and/or spared: is it the illegitimate Ishmael born of Hagar or the legitimate Isaac born of Sarah? And furthermore: what does it mean that, in the Koran, Abraham *dreams* of the sacrifice (instead of receiving the order directly from God)? Does the dream express the unconscious desire of the sacrificing Father to possess the son, in all senses of the term, to *have* him and abolish him, rather than an order come from outside, from Allah? Or, on the contrary, does the dream wish to soften the reality of the immolation and murder ("It was just a dream")? The text does indeed avoid "going into" the question of the murder of the originary Father.

Clearly, these "details" structure the *subject* very differently in each of the three monotheistic religions: in his ambiguous relation to the Law and to the bonds between men as well as to the sadomasochistic pleasure taken in the murder of the other, in the putting to death of the child in oneself, and even in one's own death.

I come back to your question now. Islam was to remain outside this trend toward a more thorough examination of the *hatelove* of and for the father that we find in Christianity. And this is not merely because of a possible fidelity to Aristotle. The contact with Aristotelianism has concealed the fact that Islam cut itself off from Jewish and Christian monotheism, in ruling out any idea of *paternity* in its idea of the divine, along with many other vital points of the biblical-Gospel canon having to do with the *loving bond* between Creator and creatures. So, for instance, original sin doesn't exist in Islam (guilty of having listened to Satan, Adam and Eve are expelled from Paradise, but their sin is not visited upon their children; furthermore, the sacredness of the Koran was revealed exclusively to Mohammed: Jews and Christians received, according to the sacred text, only a partial revelation, which they deformed.

If I insist upon these differences, it is because I suspect you'd like to know where the principal difference lies, the one that renders difficult or even impossible some encounter with Islam in the present context. To say that this difference comes from an aggravation of "Aristotelianism" prevents us questioning the *specificity* that, in my view, the bond between the believer and Islamic divine authority constitutes—a bond tantamount to a juridical pact—which is quite different from the bond between a paternal Creator whose role is to *elect* (in Judaism, whose spirit, however legalistic, does not in the least suppress the creationist value that summons God's chosen people to the work of reflection and interrogation) or *to love* (in Christianity, even in the test of abandonment and the passion). Of course, Sufism, and especially Ibn Arabi (1165–1240), introduced some subtle changes in the domain of the "great sacrifices," which this order interprets as a sacrifice of self, the *nafs* or psyche, in its face to face with nothingness. I fear, however, that certain distinctive features of Islam, outlined above, make an Islamic theo-*logy* improbable if not impossible and, similarly, any "discussion" between Sunnis and Shiites, not to mention with the other two monotheisms. These distinctive features also handicap a possible opening of Islam toward the ethical and political problems raised by the freedoms, full of risks, of the men and women of the third millennium and by the different ways of thinking in confrontation on these subjects.

All the more reason not to throw up our arms before the terrifying, even terroristic, drift of these underlying currents of Islam, but to try to draw upon the most open of them and upon the anthropological, sociological, and even psychoanalytic research today devoted to Islam, before envisaging the eventuality of mutual understanding.

THE JEWISH-CHRISTIAN DUO

We do, however, take note that the fertilization of Christian theology by Aristotle, Thomas Aquinas, and up to Hegel, gives it a hermeneutic capacity that, if it is attentive to Pope John Paul II's repentance, is today trying to propose new theological interpretations of the relations between the Jewish and Christian branches of monotheism, in terms of coexistence, if not unity. I am thinking, for example, of the current revision of the old Catholic aspiration to be the "true religion." We know the spectacular appropriation of the biblical text by patrology, which saw it as merely a "precursor" text, a simple prefiguration, a pre"modeling" ("figure" comes from *fingere* = "to model"), by definition "imperfect" and needing to be "destroyed" or "eliminated" in order to liberate its final meaning, its Hegelian *Aufhebung*, in the person of the Resurrected Christ. The now famous book by Erich Auerbach, *Figura* (1938), dismantled this "figural" imperialism characteristic of the Christian reading of the Bible. Attentive to Christian specificity, but contrary to the traditional "figural" interpretation of the "Jewish-Christian" couple, some commentators propose, as a start, a *literal rereading* of the Gospels. This approach allows them to demonstrate first of all that the Gospels pick up and develop the biblical formulations, authorizing an interpretation capable of finding its way toward a restoration of the foundational biblical message right in the heart of the New Testament: not only in order to better understand the continuity between the two components of the Jewish-Christian duo, but in order to inaugurate a possible coexistence or even a kind of unity between the upholders of the Ancient Covenant and those of the New. Isn't Jesus, in the Epistle of Paul to the Hebrews, described as a "great high priest" "forever, according to the order of Melchizedek" (Hebrews 4:14; 5:6)? In this perspective, the Pauline foundation itself, which split Christianity from Judaism, though it is not challenged, is rethought and might presage a unifying dynamic respectful of the differences between the two communities of believers, Jewish and Christian. Giorgio Agamben, in Italy, comes to grip with these problems in *The Remaining Time,* and, in yet another way, Antoine Guggenheim in France, in *Grand Prêtre de l'Ancienne et de la Nouvelle Alliance.*

If, on the other hand, Islam seems far from a possible interpretive reconsideration of its history and the resemblances-differences of its membership in the monotheistic continent, the present political-economic reasons for such an impossibility must not hide the structural difficulties that constitute it. This is why it is the job of those who read religion as an *analyzable given*—anthropologists, sociologists, psychoanalysts—with or without the specialists in religion, to try whatever approaches might help bridge the differences they have noticed and interpreted in their anthropological consequences. Utopic? Or the only possible way, given the present "clash of religions"?

Be that as it may, the fundamentalist stagnation of Islam raises a more general question about the very structure of *homo religiosis*. The latter can move beyond the *hatelove* that keeps him going only by taking a step to the side: by taking himself as object of thought. By developing his theo-logy, by forcing it to confront the plural interpretations of his need to believe, the multiple variants of his needs to believe. Is this not what Freud did when he claimed it is possible to tell the love of the other, infinitely; to analyze oneself in analyzing it, infinitely? Might psychoanalysis be one of the variations of theology? Its ultimate variation, *hic et nunc?*

But the West seems to want war too. The Crusades of the past start up again in the guise of the new crusaders of good against evil. And it is in fact Europe, more or less secularized, that invented totalitarianism.

Religious fundamentalism does not spare Christianity, of course, and this tendency appears to be fairly widespread in the United States, in a certain neoconservative Protestantism. But one may ask whether Catholicism itself, after Jean Paul II and despite its humanitarian developments, not to mention its concern for repentance, is not tempted by a defensive stiffening of its identity: as if the survival of the Catholic faith "depended" upon jihad, to the point of searching for its authenticity by falling back upon its own kinds of conservatism. Let's hope, all the same, that this won't go so far as an "identification with the aggressor"!

But to come to secularization and the Shoah. Hannah Arendt strongly emphasized, in *The Origins of Totalitarianism* and elsewhere, the new phase of anti-Semitism encouraged in Europe by multiple causalities, as well as by the "assimilation" of the Jews in the wake of the Enlightenment. The philosopher–political scientist drew back horrified by the unthinkable horror of extermination camps such as Auschwitz, or the Gulag; she concluded in substance that only "the terrified imagination can bear witness to this." Since this year commemorates the hundredth anniversary of Arendt's birth, I would like to say how honored I was to receive Rome's Amelia Rosselli Prize for my book on Hannah Arendt. To which is now added the "Hannah Arendt International Prize for Political Thought," created by the Länder of Bremen in Germany, which I intend to offer to an association devoted to Afghan women, today deprived of a political arena and led by despair to immolate themselves in fire. Because Arendt thought that the "central idea of politics" is to be able to *appear*, with one's own history, before the plurality of human bonds, because otherwise violence decrees the superfluity of life. And because I prefer that these women have access to the fires of sublimation rather than die by setting fire to themselves . . .

NEITHER SECULARIZATION, NOR TRANSCENDENTALISM

You will recall that, in stigmatizing secularization, Arendt attacked the reduction of human differences to the general term of *zoon politikon,* become generic "Man" in a reductive understanding of "human rights." In so doing, she more or less deliberately "forgot" the profusion of bodies, desires, and languages that flowered, notably during the French Enlightenment. A fortunate "oversight," however, which allowed her to denounce indefatigably the tour de force of the *assimilation* of the Jews that transformed Judaism into "Jewishness" and reduced the Jewish human being to a "pariah," opening the way to an unprecedented denial of the meaning of life and the systematic destruction of the "superfluity of human life" proclaimed and pro-grammed by the Nazis, culminating in the extinction of six million European Jews.

However, when Waldemar Gurian and Eric Voegelin, of the important political science department at the University of Notre Dame in Indiana, attempted to associate Arendt with their thesis, according to which totalitarianism is more the product of modern atheism than of a sociohistorical process, or even of the "spiritual disease of agnosticism," Arendt did not dismiss the idea that a cer-tain atheism might have contributed to the end of ethics. But she maintained that the phenomenon of totalitarianism is unique and that none of the previous factors, whether they went back to the Middle Ages or to the eighteenth century, could be called totalitar-ian. She took care as well to differentiate between her philosophical inquiry and any kind of religious position, relating the political use of the "divine" back to the insidious nihilism that she was combating: "Those who conclude from the terrible events of our time that we must go back to religion for political reasons seem to me to show as much lack of faith in God as their opponents."

One can understand then that while she was indignant, along with Bernard Lazare, about the "pariah" status that the European Enlightenment reserved for the Jews, and while elucidating its tragic destiny, up to and including the figure of the "exceptional Jew" in Kafka, Chaplin, or Stefan Zweig; or yet again while emphasizing the "temptation of suicide" as the only deliverance for "us refugees," after the radical evil perpetrated by the Europeans, which was "banal" not because it was insignificant but because it was the result "of a terribly widespread obedience and incapacity to think," Arendt refused to consider that the "spiritual inheritance of the Jews" might be sim-ply the "monopoly of the Rabbis" or that it could be reduced to a "withered erudition" set in motion by "a preoccupation with conser-vation." Moreover, she suggested, were not the artists and intellectuals of Europe, or even worldwide these days, themselves reduced to pariahs, except on rare occasions for certain rare individuals who become "stars," which is also alienating? And she concludes with this thought, whose provocative modernity I would like to shout out: "All the European nations have become pariah peoples, they are all forced to accept at new costs the struggle for liberty and the rights of all. For the first time, our destiny/the destiny of the Jewish people/is not an exceptional destiny, for the first time our struggle is the same as the European struggle for liberty. As Jews we want to fight for the liberty of the Jewish people for: 'If I don't worry about me, who else will worry about me?' As Europeans we want to struggle for European liberty, for 'If I worry only about myself, what am I?'" (Hillel).

This defense and illustration of what we must call the "European and Jewish community" bears the stamp of its time, which is that of a struggle of a certain European resistance against Nazi Europe. Yet, whatever the personal and collective tragedies Arendt survived, throughout her oeuvre she maintains her concern to implant the roots of Israel's destiny in both the affirmation of its difference *and* in political action leading to the liberation of all men, insofar as she deemed this possible/impossible by and through the dismantling/ reformation of the European tradition at its base, that is, of onto-theology, into a new kind of political thought.

RATHER THAN A DISMANTLING:

A RADICAL REFORMATION

While Arendt tried to radically reform political authority, with her extraordinarily vital sense of judgment and her indomitable capacity for survival, the destiny of the Jewish people remained neverthe-less the permanent horizon of her ambition: whether it be explicitly named or implicit in her denunciation of the threat of an atomic third world war; or in her denunciations of the violence of an au-tomation that portended the "devastation" (*Verwüstung*) of the earth

("The politico-public space is essentially in the field of violence"; "Humanity itself may disappear from the world given the policies and the means of violence it has at its disposal"); or yet again in her description of "the shifting desert" that extends the empire of totalitarianism by depriving us of the capacity to act, think, suffer— thus taking Nietzsche's warning to an extreme ("the desert is getting bigger"); finally in her evocations of the "desolation" Heidegger scrutinized and the danger of dehumanization she herself tracked down in the vicissitudes of the work, of the works and action of *The Human Condition.*

Thirty years after her death, a new threat against Israel and the world has been added to the dangers she attempted to confront with a radical reformation of political authority; these dangers, being exacerbated, render this reformation improbable. Arendt had a presentiment of this, as she showed when she warned against underestimating the Arab world and, while she unconditionally supported the State of Israel as the sole remedy for the acosmism of the Jewish people, as a return to the "world" and to the "politics" of which history had stripped it, she was unsparing in her criticism: "They'd fled into Palestine the way one wants to shoot oneself to the moon, to escape the malice of the world." Although many of her analyses and advances strike us as more than ever prophetic, Arendt could not have foretold the hardening of Islamic fundamentalism, nor the destructive chaos that this spreads about the world confronted with the impotence of "classical" politics," with the impossibility of responding to it, and with the *apolitia,* the indifference to politics, that does respond.

It is true nonetheless that this new form of fundamentalist totalitarianism—by the desertification of the thought that characterizes it and that it imposes and by its disdain for human life, which it reduces to a superfluity to be eliminated with cold premeditation— brings us back to some essential anxieties. Indeed, and more dramatically than ever before, the present state of the world places us, with unprecedented gravity, face to face with the black sun of skepticism whose shadow never spared our political philosopher and made her wonder on several occasions whether politics still made "any sense in the end."

All the same, I shall pay homage to the Arendtian "vital sense of judgment," I'll call it a sur-vival. I don't in the least take this term as a humanist bandage for the isolation, the desolation, for the personal or political destruction. I understand that Arendt is not *only* the thinker of the dismantling. I understand her happiness in thinking that radical re-formation was possible: re-formation of the self, of a people, of political space-time. This calls for a love of the past and of the future and an extraordinary capacity for rebirth. This is well and truly the attitude Arendt adopted when she identified with De Tocqueville's phrase: "A new world needs a new kind of politics," and when, avoiding any hint of facility, she dismantled the political tradition only in order to build it anew on other foundations. "Politics deals with the community and the reciprocity of different beings"; "The ruin of politics stems from the fact that the body politic is an outgrowth of the family," whose reducing of existential needs to economic management she rejected; "Politics originates in the *space-that-is-between* men, hence in something that is *outside*-man. Hence there is no such thing as a truly political substance"; "Freedom only exists in the intermediate space proper to politics."

Is this to say that politics occupies the place of the *divine* for our political thinker? Or, as I have tried to show in my book on Arendt, do the *divine* and *being* come full circle in the disquieting opinion of the *quid,* "the who"—this single person acting within the plurality of the bonds? The *divine* and the *being,* immanent, share in, or, better, they are incarnated in this fundamentally loving and interactive narrative (hence political in the Greek sense of the term) that different men and women weave around the plural sense of their actions. Might Arendtian politics be a (the first?) politics of the incarnation? Arendt recalls in effect that, referring to Genesis (1:27), Jesus affirms the difference between the sexes ("God created them male *and* female"), which precedes and engenders human diversity as condition of intrinsically political action: whereas Saint Paul, man of the law and of salvation, prefers to say that woman was created "from man" and "for man." Might Jesus be "political" already? More political than Paul, in any case, she states. Faced with the strain of the new threats imposed by the automation of the species and religious fundamentalism conjoined, two possibilities seem to open to us as we reread Arendt:

- Either galloping depoliticization will hasten the return of the religious and reduce the political space to impotence for a long and unforeseeable length of time
- or the ongoing programming of the superfluity of human life and the fundamentalist use of the death instinct will bring about a vital awakening of the *inter-esse,* of the interdependence of different people, and a reintroduction of innovative subjectivity.

Logically, the latter likelihood calls not for a return *to* but a refoundation *of* the authority of the Greco-Judeo-Christianity that gave the world the desire for a "common world," constituted by a plurality of "who's," that Arendt points to as "the center of politics." It is up to us to reinterpret this gift.

Only a "new politics" thus enlightened can still save us.

FROM JESUS TO MOZART

(CHRISTIANITY'S DIFFERENCE)

What was your reaction when the archbishop asked you to take part in the Lenten Lectures? In your opinion, what do Christians expect from you on the subject of suffering? What has a psychoanalyst to tell us?

Very surprised, initially, to be so honored. And right away the question: why? Who is this invitation addressed to? To the woman, the teacher, the literary theorist, the psychoanalyst, the writer, the president of the National Council for the Handicapped? Very impressed, and above all intimidated, to encounter this new audience. What indeed can Catholics expect from me in the fabulous space of Notre Dame de Paris? Neither a lecture nor a specialist colloquium, still less a psychoanalytic session. Be present to their suffering as they experience it from the starting point of their faith. From their sense of suffering, which I decipher in books, which I hear in my patients and try to understand, I'd like to sketch the outlines of a kind of listening that reaches out to them, that makes contact and illuminates. Might it allow believers to find not only their own paths but also to differentiate between Christianity and other beliefs and "spiritual revivals" in the current religious conflicts? Differences that one doesn't really dare to put forward, it seems to me, in these times of global conflict. Would I dare to think aloud that Christianity, and Catholicism in particular, is not necessarily what one thinks it is? Because within "what one believes"—about suffering, for example—astonishing progress has been made that might resonate in harmony with current preoccupations? And vice versa, that modern fields of knowledge may be able to interpret in a new way the wisdom that underlies traditional dogma.[1]

My reading of Christ's Passion leads me to dream: that the true complicities to counteract a rising tide of barbarity might be constructed not only—and probably less—between Christianity and other religions tempted, these days, by fundamentalism but also between Christianity and the vision of human complexity to which I am attached, which springs from Christianity, though it is now detached from it, and aspires to elucidate the perilous paths of freedom. A search for complicity beyond rupture, via the auscultation of suffering, that will unite us.

What is suffering?

Analytical experience and my own existence have convinced me that happiness is only a kind of mourning for suffering (to paraphrase Madame de Staël, affirming that "glory is the splendid mourning for happiness"). Patients come to consult me in order to confide incommensurable suffering—before seeing that one cannot eradicate suffering, but that it is possible to cross it indefinitely: by renewing bonds, languages, creativities, having another relationship with time—a sort of rebirth, of serenity, of joy. The exile I went through at the age of twenty-four was a painful experience, even underneath the veneer of a "successful integration." The life of a woman and a mother, even with the advantages of equality, is strewn with pitfalls: the main heroine of my novel *Possession*

(1996) ends up decapitated! The neurological malady of my son has brought me closer to the world of the handicapped, who to this day are extremely isolated in our fraternal Republic. And the genre of the detective story seemed obvious to me, for, like Freud (who, at the end of his life, read detective stories), I am convinced that society is founded on crime.

But I don't have an overarching definition of suffering. Of which do we speak? That of the lovers or of the female lover? Of the jobless? The sick? The handicapped? The woman? The foreigner? The dying? Each is incommensurable, and only the individual word—I hope that of the analyst, sometimes of art—can approach their truths.

Must one have known suffering to speak of it?

To claim that one has not known suffering is quite simply to deny it. The psychic life of the speaking beings that we are is the result of a long "working out the negative": birth, separation, frustration, various kinds of lacks—so many kinds of suffering. And many of the physical kinds of suffering are inseparable from psychic pain, or are even conditioned or exacerbated by it.

Isn't suffering what makes you most doubt God's existence?

Certainly not. If I am not a believer, it is for far more complex philosophical reasons. Besides, isn't asking God to be an all powerful painkiller already a kind of nihilism? This demand in itself reduces the divine to the ups and downs of human existence.

In Christianity and in psychoanalysis, suffering does not have the same meaning. What are in your opinion their divergences and rapprochements?

Since Antiquity, the Western tradition has defined suffering negatively, as pleasure's cessation. Freud inherits this approach when he attributes psychic ill-being and its somatic disorders to the accidents of sexual life or the impasses of desire. But he completes his approach when he undertakes to analyze melancholic and depressive states and when he introduces the notion of the death drive into the unconscious alongside the pleasure principle.

From the polysemy of the word *suffering* come some inevitable intersections between the meanings given to it by psychoanalysis and Christianity. The differences between these two approaches are, however, considerable, and the main one resides in the fact that, for psychoanalysis, psychic suffering, far from being of value, is the result of repression, of resistance to pleasure, of the desire "not to want to know." Whereas Christianity begins by valorizing pain, as a necessary path toward the love of the Father: not, however, without working it out in the representation of joy, by means of sublimation (music, painting, literature) and while "sexualizing" it, more or less unconsciously, by what will later be called the sadomasochism of mortification or penitence.

Two points in common, however: the recognition of suffering as an integral part of the speaking being and the valorization of language as the royal road to traversing it, to its relief (we say *perlaboration,* or *working through,* and *sublimation*). The Council of Trent .and Baroque art later optimized this tendency inherent in Christianity from the start, which was to revolutionize modern times: Tridentine Christianity definitely extracted suffering from its victim place; it lightened suffering's plaintiveness by means of the harmony of the work of art, transforming suffering into bliss [*jouissance*]. No more than bliss can suffering tell itself directly and totally, says post-Tridentine art; they can only express themselves through transposition, displacement, ellipsis, or condensation into the flesh of words, sounds, images. Right to laughter at the suffering in oneself, right to desecrating it even by the gesture of the representation that acknowledges and tames it. Such is the distinctive mark of European culture, its counterweight to suffering. Not that this will spare it either the horrors of wars or those of the Shoah, culminating in what one today calls freedom of expression, which, along with the rights of man, remains our only response to global explosions of the death drive.

People often say Christians value suffering, that they take pleasure in it; what do you think? For example, the Beatitudes: "Blessed are those who weep," do you take this as praise of suffering?

This text has the advantage of doing away with the guilt attached to suffering, and, because of this, it may be interpreted as an extraordinary conquest of human freedom. To begin with, the Beatitudes extract suffering from its secretiveness and shame. When a depressed person lets himself weep on the couch, the psychoanalyst understands that the patient has distanced himself from suicide. Still, this removal of distress may become complacent suffering [*dolorisme*] or even a means of blackmail. On the other hand, in Christianity's history, the relation to suffering changes. Whereas St. Ignatius Loyola weeps a lot, Teresa of Avila is able to transform her suffering into ecstasy; she rejects nuns' propensity toward melancholy: in the exacerbated asceticism of his "little Senanque," Saint Jean of the Cross, she writes, "frightens" her.

According to you, Christianity completely changed the vision and the acceptance of suffering. In what way? What are the advances and at the same time, the limits?

Indeed, Christianity is the only religion that addresses suffering "intimately" [*la tutoie*]—that tames it—and the culture that comes along with it or after it shows the effects of this: "Hush, oh my anguish, and keep still," writes Baudelaire. "Ideas take over from chagrin," adds Proust. The recognition of the right to pain; the sharing of the suffering of others in compassion, by tactful words and even in social activism; and, at the same time, the revelation of the pleasure, "that pitiless tormentor" (Baudelaire again) that slumbers beneath the veil of malaise—to cite only three possible destinies of suffering, among the many discoveries of the literature of, or inspired by Christianity—testify to an extraordinary awareness of psychic life. Christianity did not produce a kind of "knowledge" strictly speaking about the origins and transformation of such states, but it brought them out in descriptions of unparalleled subtlety, notably those of the mystics.

The limits to this Christian suffering? Compassion runs the risk of infantilizing the sufferer by making him an object to be taken care of, rather than encouraging the political subject. Handicapped people reject this attitude to the point of denying their own suffering; they'd rather emphasize their battles than let themselves be "taken care of." Compassion is powerless confronted with what I call the new maladies of the soul: vandalism, drug addiction, grave psychosomatic problems. Moreover, suffering, inasmuch as it is a kind of violence that does not know itself, has often erupted in the form of morbid rituals or been turned upside down into vengeful cruelty, the persecution of heretics and bloody religious wars.

Yet the lucidity of testimonies in which the pathos of the unbearable is soothed into the musical rightness of a style respectful of the limits of the sharable remains a precious heritage of the Christian tradition. While making use of the discoveries of biology or genetics, the modern accompaniment to suffering owes it to itself to analyze this heritage as well, so as to be more capable of analyzing (in the etymological sense of the word *analyze,* that is, "to dissolve," "to deconstruct") new kinds of suffering. Which calls for an increasing subtlety in our interpretation and hence in our methods of accompanying suffering.

On the other hand, Catholic culture nowadays seems rather indifferent to this concern. It prefers to adopt degraded forms of compassion, which, in the absence of religious decency and with exaggerated voyeurism, are perverted by a flood of miserabilism and "reality shows." A left-wing daily paper wanted to know why I work with the National Council for the Handicapped. I reminded them of my work with the physically and mentally handicapped at the Bonneuil pilot school, at the La Borde Clinic, at the Cité Universitaire hospital, the Salpêtrière, and my personal experience as ·a mother and psychoanalyst: this didn't suffice, I had to "tell all," I had to "expand on that suffering." I have become an activist for the handicapped, I ended up saying, so that the question, "why this commitment," will not ever again be put to me. Is this a question they ask a person who fights racism, anti-Semitism, or social marginalization? Two centuries of the "rights of man" render the struggle against those sorts of suffering *natural;* does one still need to dramatize the suffering of the handicapped, rather than give an account of the concrete work we do in order to guarantee equal opportunities for all, whatever his or her suffering? As you may have gathered, this interview has never been published.

No, I have not forgotten that we are speaking of the Christian idea of suffering and its secular substitutes. But, unlike Freud, I don't say that religion is merely an illusion and source of neurosis. The time has come to recognize, without being afraid of "scaring off" either the faithful or the agnostics, that the history of Christianity is a preparation for humanism. Of course, humanism is in a state of rupture with Christianity, but it starts from it: a "rupture" that Christianity heralded in being the only religion that comes within a hair's breadth of exiting from the domain of the religious, notably— but not only—when it makes God himself suffer to death. Does this "hiatus" (Urs von Balthasar) of the divine take suffering as sacred or, on the contrary, does it deconsecrate it? It is well and truly from under the cupolas of Christian churches that suffering rises in sonorous variations that soothe us, or even resuscitate us for good, and it can even manifest itself in carnival laughter on the squares of the very churches themselves. Is it not from within Christianity that Dante wrote his prayer in the form of a "divine comedy"? Even humanism will only avoid the dead ends of its rationalism if it allows itself to interpret such antecedents in depth.

At times it seems that certain parts of your text could have been written by a Christian. How do you feel about such a remark? Why does Christ's suffering touch you so?

Your comment would have pleased my father immensely. A member of the Orthodox faith, he studied theology before he studied medicine. And the proper noun *Kristev* means "of the cross."

More seriously, Christ is the only god who suffers and who dies—before resuscitating. One may, like Nietzsche, prefer Dionysus's drunkenness. I myself think that by making its God a Man who suffers, Christianity announces its discovery, which is that depression is an indispensable and decisive stage of thought (this is what the "depressive position," prelude to the acquisition of language in the child, demonstrates). It tells us also that suffering is the flip side of creative exaltation (in the artist, for example). Need [*le manque*] is thenceforth inscribed in the being, in the Supreme Being itself, and in any reaching for the Absolute. This is not *declinology*, before the invention of the term, but a formidable liberation of the conditions and the capacity to think! It was necessary to internalize violence into suffering, sound its depths and its delights, to remove the passion from it finally, by integrating it into "amorous intelligence," into the "infinite intellectual love" by which God loves himself, right to his suffering to death (to borrow Spinoza's definition of the divine).

You see, in trying to plumb the mysteries of Christianity starting from analytical experience, but also starting from philosophy, art, and literature, which very often precede it, it appears, in effect, that Christ leads to Mozart: that Christianity refines suffering into joy. Listen to the Miserere Nobis of the *Mass in C Minor*: the sacrifice resolves itself into serenity, then ecstasy. What an unexpected filiation! Allah's madmen, among others, should give this some thought.

Can psychoanalysis explain suffering?

Psychoanalysis neither explains nor judges; it is content to transform. Yes, it happens, now and then it happens, it's an art, a vocation for the analyst as for the analysand. This alchemy presupposes that I associate myself with the other's suffering, that I project myself into him and that simultaneously I dissociate myself so as to interpret his malaise, different from mine, and only thus do I give the sufferer turned analysand a provisional meaning, which lets him start over. The exchange of transference and countertransference strikes me as a modern variation of the act of pardon, let us write *par-don* [bygift]. The suffering, like the bad [*le mal*], suffered or inflicted, is not effaced, but from now on both are part of my capacity to think and to share, thus to create. A sort of rebirth.

Do you think women have a greater capacity to bear suffering?

Feminine masochism is not an unanalyzable datum, since it is the story of the patrilineal family, which has subordinated the anatomical difference of the sexes to paternal authority and to the overvaluing of male sexuality. Yet, even under these circumstances, women live their suffering less in the obsessive fear of death than in the time of rebeginnings, of openings out. They adapt to suffering, they distil it all the way to suicide (like Virginia Woolf), but they are also able to strip it of its passion by an immersion in the "pure and the impure" of the world (like Colette). Which men in their way know how to do . . . as long as they don't lose sight of their own femininity. On this plane as well, the mystics were precursors, like certain writers (such as Joyce).

Have you accepted suffering because of a potential benefit? Have you refused suffering that struck you as absurd?

I don't accept suffering, I try to transmute it. Take an amorous disappointment: I have never dreamed of compensating via the material, intellectual, or spiritual "benefit" that the relation in question might have offered. What to do then, since any kind of enthusiasm—and love is one—ultimately unveils its limits and its lacks? Above all, not lock suffering up in the trap of a trade for some imagined "good." But ask oneself, for example, if the pain is not the twin sister of the excessive idealization. The malaise then fades away following its own logic rather than simmering on the back burner in "acceptance" or calling for revenge in a separation full of hate. The "good," in this context, can only be moving beyond the suffering, its exhaustion by means of thought or sublimation. If I consider that writing a book, for example, is a good, good for me, whatever the deprivations involved, I don't take them as suffering. On the other hand, even from adolescence, I refused the absurd suffering imposed on me by the country of my birth in order to adhere to the so-called communist ideal and I took the part of de-Stalinization by joining the "dissidents"—not without peril. It never occurred to us that the Berlin wall might fall.

"SUFFERING"

(LENTEN LECTURES, MARCH 19, 2006)

Thank you, dear Anne-Marie Pelletier. I thank you all, moreover, for the honor you do me in offering me the opportunity to speak within the prestigious framework of these Lenten Lectures.[1]

We could not open the discussion, *here and now,* around the terrible and familiar theme of "suffering," without mentioning Job and Rachel; we owe it to ourselves to evoke the horror of the Shoah. And so you have done, Madam, with your sense of religious and political history, in which I thought I noticed the "repentance" of Jean Paul II that so marked me. Therefore I shan't come back to these essential themes.

Speak *of* suffering, speak *suffering?*—you were saying, and I heard Baudelaire's "Recueillement": "My suffering, give me your hand, come over here." These words are neither an invitation to silence nor an acquiescence in what is unnameable. Here we are, along with the author of the *Fleurs du mal,* at the heart of Catholic experience and the art that goes with it, or detaches itself from it, that—for the first time in the world—permit themselves to address suffering as an intimate [*tutoyer la douleur*]: by extracting it from the secretiveness in which shame blushes, by separating it from the complaint in which resentment [*ressentiment*] moans, traversing the scandal where fear disguised as anger rumbles.

It is indeed this Christly therapy of malaise, through the musical subtlety of the utterance, through social justice, and through the "beyond," of which I would like to speak, developing Anne-Marie Pelletier's thoughts.

You have before you, ladies and gentlemen, a woman who is not a believer—a psychoanalyst, teacher, writer—convinced nonetheless that the "genius of Christianity" has introduced and continues to diffuse radical innovations as concerns the religious experience of speaking beings. Innovations whose revealing and, in this sense, revolutionary and wide-ranging effects we have not done taking the measure of and that Christians themselves do not dare recognize or make recognizable as "Christian difference" in today's conflict of religions.

Among the specific innovations, that which concerns suffering may be the most radical, for it is, paradoxically, the least mysterious and hence more universal. Let me explain myself.

Christ's suffering on the Cross—which cannot but strike you, and me, during this period of Lent, which holds human beings in thrall at Easter, preceding the Resurrection—Christ's suffering, therefore, is neither of the same order, nor as mysterious as that which faith confronts when it touches upon the virgin birth of the Man God, nor that other mystery, which touches upon faith, of the Resurrection. Between these two poles of the Incarnation (Immaculate Conception of Marie by Anne, her mother, and virginal birth of Jesus by the grace of the Holy Spirit), and of the Resurrection of the Son of God on the Father's right hand, and the promise of the resurrection of all bodies, the *suffering of Jesus,* however paroxysmal it may be, is nonetheless sharable and, in this sense, common.

The fact is there: "A scandal for the Jews, madness for the Greeks," the suffering and the death of the Man God are charged with a complexity that the history of Christianity has not ceased to ponder, and at the same time refine, and that does not fail to amaze the modern human being that I am. I shall focus on three aspects:

To suffer physically *and* morally: tortured body *and* spiritual abandonment; flagellation-crucifixion on one side, "My Father, why have you abandoned me?" and on the other: the Crucified Christ is open to the excesses of suffering [*dolorisme*] while simultaneously offering unprecedented consolation. Such are the benefits and traps of *compassion*.

But doesn't the annulment of Christ in his descent into hell annul God himself along with the Son? This question has not been avoided in Christian history, nor will it be today: so true does it remain that the "death of God" may be understood as not just a nihilistic catastrophe but also a condition sine qua non of his "eternal return." Return of the religious or return of the "sacred"? Such will be my second line of questioning, around what I shall call the *sovereign suffering*, which Greek uses the term *kénose* to designate.

Last, what is this "intellectual and infinite love" with which God loves himself in the suffering of his Son, with which he loves himself right to his own suffering, before making this Son rise again in a new reconciliation, if it is not *sublimation*? If it is not the traversing of suffering in thought's serenity, in the deployment of the arts: a sort of joy? This will be my third point.

- Compassion,
- sovereign suffering,
- sublimation.

Three versions of suffering, faced with suffering, traversing suffering.

1. Condemned as a rebel, even as a criminal, subjected to crucifixion, the most shameful of chastisements, Christ, however, does not experience his physical and mental suffering as a punishment—as a sin punished by the law. This *innocence of the suffering* announces, from the Last Supper on, a special status for suffering within Christianity, in that pain, and death, are to be henceforth seen as a *necessary point of passage* of the Christian message centered upon the Word and Word of Love. In letting himself be crucified, Jesus says in substance that suffering is inherent in the reconciliation of the human with the divine. How to understand this suffering that is not dictated from without but inherent in the cohabitation of the human and the divine: inherent in the fact that Christian man is a Man of pain-and-of-love? This postulate has so permeated Western culture that we no longer even think of referring it back to Jesus when it pops up under the pen of a writer. In *La Chanson of Roland,* for example: "The man has learned much who has suffered much." Or in Ronsard: "I want to trace the pain that I endure: / in one hundred pages harder than diamond, / so that the race of the future / may judge how in loving I have suffered." And, in La Fontaine, the familiar: "Better to suffer than to die, is the motto of men."[2] So that the Enlightenment, in its attempt to shake off divine authority, even attacked suffering and in its place put . . . happiness, far more than reason; in Diderot, whom I quote: "There is only one duty; this is to be happy";[3] or Rousseau: "As the first step toward the good is not to do bad, so the first step toward happiness is not to suffer."[4] But is this possible? The same Rousseau writes, this time in a letter to Madame de Saint-Germain: "I hope that one day they will judge what I was by the fact that I knew how to suffer."

Innocent, absolved of guilt, flesh bruised and spiritually wanting ("Eli, Eli, lama sabachthani?" Mark 15:34)—what solitude has not been haunted by this cry and this silence!—Christian suffering is *sharable*: this is the first way in which Christianity has effected a revolution in the approach to suffering. Sharable, first of all, between humans and Christ, who, in assuming it, confers upon it extraordinary dignity, at the interface of the human and the divine; sharable, next, and consequently, among human beings themselves, who only allow themselves to look for a way to relieve it on the condition that they can look it in the face, give it a name, and interpret it.

Of this complex alchemy Christianity has practiced by rendering suffering sacred the better to deconsecrate it, but only through its *sublimation,* as we say in psychoanalysis, we generally retain the idea of a *consoling Christ:* who identifies with the malaise of men and continuously offers them the mirror of his suffering onto which to project their own. It is indeed in the revolving door of this sharing, by dying like a man for men, that Jesus removes their sin and Evil from the world. Still, we know that this communication of suffering to suffering, this passionate contagion, this *com-passion* (to suffer with the others, my peers [*mes semblables*]) can be—and was—interpreted in two ways.

a) The recommendation of suffering as the unavoidable path to salvation was transformed into an eroticized suffering (*invested,* in psychoanalytical terms), within which mortification rituals find their place: "I" exist if, and only if, I suffer; the feeling of pain alone makes me exist; it is pain that makes my existence meaningful; without it, my being would lack employment, utter boredom. The analytic experience is very familiar with such "dolorist" states: in sadomasochism, but also in a complacent kind of depressiveness, as in "marginal states" close to psychosis.

b) On the other hand, however, com-passion brings about a historically unprecedented moral solidarity with vulnerable humankind. For two thousand years, right up to the most recent Christian humanism, Christian morality comes to drink at the source of this compassion, and one can only salute the generosity of the works that put this compassion into practice. I have seen for myself, notably in the care for the handicapped, the extraordinary vitality of Christians, and Christian institutions dedicated to compassion, that courageously supplement the weaknesses of legislator and politics. I have even perceived the limits of this approach, with its attendant risk of infantilizing people who are thus excluded from social history as suffering objects to be looked after. One can understand, then, that, starting with Diderot and his 1749 *Lettre sur les aveugles à l'usage de ceux qui voient* [Letter on the blind for the use of those who see], men and women of handicap, and their families, refuse the charitable and compassionate attitude and involve themselves in a political struggle that demands equality as a political right for everyone. All the same, realizing this political solidarity requires mental solidarity between those who suffer from various kinds of exclusion and those who have been relatively spared. This co-presence at the suffering of others, indispensable in order to "change the gaze" and put such solidarity into effect, sends us back to the constitutive vulnerability of we human beings at the junction of biology and meaning. We are, however, forced to admit that Christian humanism, when it does not lock itself into redemptive suffering [*dolorisme*], prepares the believer to acknowledge this vulnerability in himself, the better to share the political struggles of those who suffer. How many of those who claim to believe in Republican fraternity are these days capable of this?

2. However, in only attending to the humanist—as I would call it—aspect of Christian suffering, one overlooks other advances that revolutionize even metaphysics itself.

Jesus assumes human nature up to its most extreme physical (flagellation, the putting to death of the body) and moral (abandonment by God the Father, the loss of the Spirit) limits, the better to raise it up again in the divine, to reconcile human nature with the divine. Transposing this acceptance of his onto the anthropological plane, I would say that Jesus, suffering because desiring and thinking beyond the possible and the finite, offers an experience in which we recognize our own desires and thoughts, by definition without any possibility of satisfaction: forever unfulfilled, forever doubled by anguish, constituted in the process of incomplete maturation of the human by a series of separations, of prohibitions and renunciations, of modulation of the drives and of sublimation of the pleasures. Each of us suffers if and because we think "beyond," Christ's message seems to say, and I shall be more specific, "through" the body; which implies that thought is an accompaniment and a traversal of the anguish. So another *experience of thinking* shows itself in Christianity, which is not thought-calculation, thought-judgment, or thought-adaptation, but the thought co-present with pleasure, all the way to *suffering.*

For years I listened, on the psychoanalytic couch, to a sensitive, cultivated, and intelligent person who complained of being "incapable of writing." She took a long time to understand that what was blocking her did not in the least come from her difficulty in plumbing the cumbersome wealth of her person, but rather from her total incapacity to forget about herself, to come out of herself. Painful, to be sure, this narcissistic and more generally psychological annulment: but is this not the condition for thinking, creating, writing?

What are the modalities, ancient or modern, of the traversal of suffering? I shall return to this question before I conclude; meanwhile, I suggest that we go one step further.

Does Jesus in his suffering speak only to human nature? Son of God, but allowing himself to be annihilated, does he not turn the divine itself to nothing? Theological debates leave the question open. Is it possible to take it up again today? The suffering to death, pinpointed by Saint Paul, designates Christ's experience of the limits, of the lowering, of the humiliation, of the inanition. The question remains: is the *suffering to death* only due to Christ's humanity, or does it affect the very nature of his divinity? And thus of Divinity? After the Last Supper, and right before the Passion, doesn't Christ tell Philip: "He that hath seen me hath seen the Father"?[5] Protestants and Orthodox apparently attend more closely to this "descent" (of the Father himself) "into the lowest earthly regions."[6] The Greek language designates it by the noun *kénose,* which greatly marked my childhood and signifies "not-being," "nothing," "inanity," "nullity"—but also "absurd," "misleading" (the adjective *kénose* signifies "empty," "useless," "vain," the verb *kenoun* "empty," "cut," "annihilate"). To admit to the inanity of the human cannot but affect the divine itself, if it is true that "He who descended is the very one who ascended,"[7] and that he is the consubstantial image of God: "All things were created by him and for him."[8]

This is why I say that God himself is "in sufferance" in Christian suffering, and that this scandal, which theology hesitates to confront, prefigures modern times' confrontation with the "death of God." "God is dead, God himself is death" is a prodigious, terrible representation, "which submits to representation scission's deepest abyss."[9] But also, what therapeutic power! What a prodigious restoration of the capacity to think and to desire in this rude exploration of suffering right to the point of losing the spirit along with the body, the suffering to death! It is because the Father and the Spirit themselves are mortal, made nothing by the Man of suffering's intermediary, the Man who thinks all the way to his suffering to death of their rebirth. Thought may rebegin: might this be the ultimate form of freedom that Christian suffering thus proclaims? Nietzsche did not fail to point out that this letting himself go all the way to *kénose* gives the *human and divine* death on the cross "this freedom, this sovereign detachment [which places suffering] above any kind of resentment."[10]

For the interruption, even momentary, of the bond that links Christ to his Father and to life, this caesura, this "hiatus,"[11] offers not merely an image but also a story for certain psychic cataclysms that lie in wait for the presumed balance of each individual and, because of this, make a dressing for them [*les pansent*]. Each and every one of us is the result of a long "work on the negative": birth, weaning, separation, frustration. For having staged this rupture at the very heart of the absolute subject, Christ, for having presented it in the figure of a Passion, as the other, supportive side of the resurrection, Christianity brings to consciousness the essential internal dramas of each person's becoming. It thus gives itself an immense . . . unconscious . . . cathartic power. It took the long development of the sciences, and especially the human sciences, all the way to Freud's psychoanalytic leap, to progress toward the psychosexual interpretation of these variations upon suffering. A long road of which we know only, for the time being, the beginning.

And what if it were only through *kénose* that the divine could most beautifully return to the consciousness of its rebeginning? "Most beautifully" for, next to com-passionate suffering, *kénose's* sovereign suffering, paradoxically, is an emptying of passion: it de-eroticizes suffering. Moreover, the absolute necessity for the human spirit to aspire to the Other, desire the divine, want to seize meaning, is suddenly revealed to be empty, vain, useless, absurd. It is even through this co-presence of the absolute-and-the-nothingness of desire that Christianity reaches the limits of the religious. I would therefore say that with *kénose* we are no longer confronted with the religious but with the *sacred,* understood as a traversal, via thought, of the unthinkable: nothingness, the useless, the vain, the absurd. To the *sacred,* which it is modern knowledge's ambition to approach—fully aware of what is at stake. Mysticism already took the risk of getting close to these realms; in the voice of Meister Eckhart: "I ask God to leave me free of God." But it may be Jean of the Cross who best announced this presence of the impossible in the tension of desire and thought, this nothingness that stresses the "vain pursuit"[12] that goes along with the need to believe.

3. Compassionate or sovereign, Christ's suffering is both a physical suffering and a psychic abandonment, I repeat, that is nonetheless resolved in the *reconciliation.* And it is Spinoza who lets the modern person interpret this ultimate mystery: "God loves himself with infinite intellectual love," he writes in *Ethics* 5,[13] thus translating what

is, for the believer, a resorption of the suffering into the "new body" of Christ "ascended" to the right of his Father, on the one hand, and into the "promise" of resurrection, on the other. Because this "infinite intellectual love" cohabits with the existential pain that it elucidates, it is called God and it is a joy. Hence I say that, for having emphasized, as never before, com-passion and *kénose* as doubles inseparable from "amorous intelligence," the genius of Christianity promoted a formidable *counterweight to suffering* (in the two forms that I evoked: dolorism, with its cortege of supportive morality, and the death of God) that is none other than *its sublimation or its working through* by psychic and verbal activity. "I," suffering being because desiring/ thinking, loving/loved, am able to *represent* my passion to myself, and this *representation* is my resurrection. My spirit, in love with the passion, recreates it in the creations of the loving intellect: thoughts, stories, paintings, music come out of this.

Thus, in inscribing suffering as an internal element of the amorous bond with the loving Father and, consequently, with human beings themselves, Christianity does not limit itself to eroticizing malaise—which it also does; it intends suffering to be shared, which means that it dedicates suffering to a kind of thinking indissociable from the amorous imagination. There is no act of love susceptible of consoling suffering if it is not preceded by speech, by imagination, by transference/countertransference between consoled and consoler. This is what Christianity tries to do when it recognizes the desperate orientation (this *version*) toward the ideal Father of psychic suffering, which aggravates all other kinds of suffering; this is what Christianity tries to do especially when it transforms this *père-version* into creativity, into sublimation, into the art of living.

Let us recall John of the Cross who explores the inaccessibility of the divine in the pure suffering of that which he calls the "vain pursuit" of the need to believe. And—very close to him, but how different—Teresa of Avila, who transforms this pain into a kind of bliss [*jouissance*] experienced as an "ecstasy," when it is not an audacious meddling in the politics of the Church so as to refound the Carmelite Order, which this woman writer hands on to us in the splendor of what she calls her "fiction."

At the same period, in response to the Protestant Reformation and the humanist breakthrough, Baroque art following the Council of Trent breathes new life into the Catholic experience through the fabulous proliferation of music, painting, literature. Without denying the suffering, nor leaving out the silence, new languages sublimate plaintiveness, turning it into a kind of serenity ready to bloom with joy. Doesn't *Ecce homo* here arrive at total lucidity in a new *ecceitas,* that is, in a singularity already foretold by Duns Scotus, but one that is henceforth none other than *the singular freedom of creation* of European men and women, living through misfortune and wretchedness and initiating a new, a modern universality? Let—I invite you as my final argument—let the Miserere Nobis of Mozart's *Mass in C Minor* resonate in your mind. *Miserere nobis,* sings the choir, and pain is here refined into complicity, into grace, into glory.

This civilization—from the Christ who inhabits this altar to Mozart whose renown is worldwide—this civilization, ours, today menaced from the outside and by our own inability to interpret and renew it, bequeaths us thus its subtle triumph over human suffering, transformed, without losing sight of the suffering to death of the divine itself. It is incumbent on us to take up this heritage once again, to give it meaning, and to develop it in the face of the current explosions of the death drive.

Totalitarian regimes and, in a different, but symmetrical way, the modern automation of the species, claim to put an end to, eradicate, or ignore suffering, the better to force it upon us as means of exploitation or manipulation. The only alternative to these different forms of barbarism founded on the denial of malaise is to work through distress again and again: as we try to do, as you try to do.

Differently, and very often each *against* the others. Against or "right against"?

Still, when new barbarians, having lost even the capacity to suffer, strew pain and death around and in us; when poverty grows by leaps and bounds in the global world, face to face with extravagant accumulations of wealth, which doesn't care, aren't compassion and sublimation not much help? Of course. What I do know, however, is that no political action could step in for them if the humanism—itself a kind of suffering—didn't give itself the means to interpret and reinvent this "loving intelligence" that comes and is inseparable from the Man of pain and suffering's compassion that might be confused with the divine itself. Such is the challenge of the planetary era, which I receive as an exciting and long-term vocation, and which we will not be able to take up unless we try to think and act together, as these Lenten Lectures invite us to.

THE GENIUS OF CATHOLICISM

In life as in death, Jean Paul II was not a reformist. He was content to reveal, to a dumbfounded, global world, the genius of Catholicism. This is extraordinary, in these times of nihilistic distress and its maniacal underside, fundamentalism.[1]

Paradoxically, this man of faith was not universally heeded when he proclaimed his faith in the "rights of man." Pronounced in French, with his Polish accent and a delectable dash of slyness, the expression today makes extraordinary sense, initiating the everlasting exit of religion check by jowl with the ongoing emergence of humanism.

Since God is unconscious, and the clash of civilizations reveals the truth of metaphysics, today unleashed and unbridled, in the global rise of technology and the stock market bubble, we in the West wondered what a pope could do. Jean Paul II had the genius to turn the most generous elements of Catholicism against the drifting off course of this very metaphysics, to which his faith belonged, so as to embody an unprecedented, spectacular, and peace-bringing resistance. When he said, to the anguish of the peoples crushed by Stalinian totalitarianism, "Don't be afraid!" this is the voice of a two-thousand-year-old theology, careful to recognize each conscience, suddenly transformed into a political act. It opened a breach in the Berlin Wall before the economy finished off the job.

When he took to laughing and singing along with millions of young people during the Catholic festivals, he was a loving father/ one (who is) missing from broken families, offering himself up to the longing of teenagers. These happenings couldn't take place before sexual liberation, the emancipation of women, the pill, abortion, the abyss of AIDS, I knew. When Jean Paul II without hesitation reincarnated himself as a therapist betting on sublimation, or maybe on repression, when he believed that the spirit's enthusiasm could tame the appetites of the flesh, we understood that he wasn't modern. So was he postmodern? When he condemned excessive liberalism, fundamentalism, and the new crusades, perplexed, we met up with him once more on the same side of the geopolitical chessboard as the French president and the so-called developing nations.

Did he want us to think that liberty, along with the rights of man, were Catholic? In May 2002 I had a chance to get close to him, in Sofia, in the country of my birth, his visit coinciding with the celebration of the Cyrillic alphabet. There Jean Paul II expressed what has always seemed to me an urgent necessity, that no policy maker had glimpsed: an enlarged Europe could not be constituted without reconciling Western Churches and Eastern Orthodoxy. A subtle historian and optimistic strategist, Jean Paul II reminded us that Bulgaria opposed the deportation of the Jews as demanded by the Nazis during the Shoah and that the mutual comprehension established there between Jews, Christians, and Muslims might serve as example to the world. Was he going to add the nonbelievers, the atheists? I'm still waiting. It was a philosophical pope I believed I heard, finally, affirming that if we sometimes lose sight of the meaning of life, a demanding and sure way remains, nonetheless, that allows us to continue searching for it: . . . writing. Holy Writ? I doubted it! But also the experience of personal writing, he added, hitting the nail on the head, such as Saints Cyril and Methodius brought to the Slavic peoples in creating their alphabet! Really, this pope . . .

On that day, and up to his death, we saw a handicapped man expose himself. All those handicapped citizens, their families, and those with whom I work to have the rights of these excluded people, not like the others, recognized, know the difficulty, or even the impossibility of ensuring that the dignity of the most vulnerable, those who make us face up to deficiency and psychic or physical death, was respected. Whereas society, dogged by the cult of performance, of excellence and enjoyment, makes manifest the shortcomings of this culture of mutual assistance and, beyond, of the identification with the suffering of Christ on the Cross or the ease in Christian sadomasochism that Jean Paul II successfully maintained even on his deathbed, the body of the handicapped pope was and remains an invitation to know life up to its limits. And to develop this solidarity with people who are dependent—the handicapped or the aged—which modern humanism has so much difficult doing.

We would have liked him to be the apostle of women, of contraception, of sexual liberty, of condoms, of homosexuals. This was to ask him to break with Christian tradition and his own convictions. This theatrical man was nothing if not a true Catholic, capable nonetheless of revealing to us the genius of Catholicism because he himself had the genius of incarnate speech. Right away his words were gestures, images, voyages, sense and sensation, love, humor and reflection, an ongoing incarnation. We took him for a manipulator of showbiz society, and he was that too, amusing himself all the while. More deeply yet, he revealed that Catholicism is the precursor, and perhaps even the deep logic, the secretly envied pole of this show business empire that enthralls us, and in which a true Catholic like this phenomenologist in search of the Virgin Mary and Saint John of the Cross is utterly at ease. For Wojtyla the man there is no other *cor-*

pus mysticum than the universal Church whose visible and public rituals culminate in aesthetic splendor, well before the deluge of media and far superior to them.

Is there a beyond for the Catholic genius? The universal passion set off by the passage of Jean Paul II to his heavenly Father allows us to doubt it. Unless it signifies that the passion according to Jean Paul II is not a religion like the others, since it alone reaches out to men everywhere. An exit from religion, then?

Such is indeed the aftershock of the era that the conclave today faces; it must be tempted, therefore, to tighten its bonds with traditional faith by leaning on a reinforced Vatican institution and on the developing countries in their most conservative aspects. Such a choice would be doubly advantageous:

It would comfort and unify the third world, by offering it an image of a Catholicism tolerant but true to tradition, all the while engaging other religions in a competition over its model of compassion, to the detriment of its fundamentalist model.

It would constitute a challenge to humanism itself, forcing it to resign or refine its ethical ambitions before it affirms itself as the only kind of experience capable of keeping in mind both technology and the sciences, especially the biological sciences, as well as the new aspirations that arise from these, which drastically change tradition at this start of this, the third millennium.

And to say that this turn of affairs rests on the life and death of one man! *Ecce homo . . .*

DON'T BE AFRAID OF EUROPEAN CULTURE

Catholicism has managed to fashion and put the finishing touches on its mastery of show business over the centuries, but it is with Jean Paul II, in point of fact, that it has begun to reap the benefits of this in such a way as to offer itself up as Grand Master over and above any other faith. We realized that this pope was not just a very great Church dignitary: indeed it is Catholicism's difference from other religions that Karol Wojtyla displayed to a dumbstruck planet, and momentarily reconciled, on the day of his funeral.[1]

First of all, this man of deep faith—he used to define this faith along with John of the Cross as "the active night of the spirit" and, as with the mystical doctor, this faith was never purely "speculative or abstract," but possessed "a value above all vital"[2]—this pope *had a body*. The body of a skier, of an actor (he wrote that "the person is an actor"), a body touched—gravely—in an attack planned by the KGB, the body of an old man, handicapped, but, in every case, an "active body" (as he writes in his Husserl-inspired thesis),[3] and in which cohabit, indissociable, the Man of pain and suffering, child of Mary and Spinoza's joy.

I encountered him in Sofia, all but paralyzed and aphasic, all the same every fiber of his body loving keeping time to the songs and the steps of the young dancers who had come to fete him. And proclaiming that if we lose our sense of life, two sources of help still remain: *to write,* as Saints Cyril and Methodius, the inventors of the Slavic alphabet, proposed, and to forge links—not only between the Eastern and Western Churches but also between Christians, Jews, and Muslims. Transcendence for him was embodied in geopolitics and writing.

When he called, in French, with his delightful Polish accent, for the respect of human rights, we who had given up waiting for Godot and who suffocated in the shadow of the Berlin Wall could hardly hold his ignorance against him, I mean his scorn for the pill, for the condom, and for blended or homoparental families. *Ecce homo* was already turning into the champion of *ecceitas,* of the liberty of each and all, proclaiming *urbi et orbi:* "Don't be afraid!" We understood we shouldn't fear Stalinian totalitarianism. The day of his funeral, which I watched on television on East 57 Street in New York, I thought I heard him say much more: "Don't be afraid of European culture." And I took up *Personne et acte* again.

In this book Jean Paul II proposes a tightly argued exploration of universal "Man," starting from "traditional philosophy" (from Aristotle to Thomas of Aquinas and Kant) as rethought by the phenomenology of Husserl's *transcendental ego,* including Roman Ingarden and even Max Scheler, without omitting the *Being and Nothingness* of Jean Paul Sartre, whom Wojtyla claimed to prefer to the logical-positivists! (29). This meant neither more nor less than "reinterpreting certain formulae proper to all this philosophy" (8) and, at the same time—this is a precious avowal—making a "personal effort . . . to arrive at this reality of the man-person seen via his acts"

(8). In what he calls his discovery of the "person via his acts," the future pope announces that he is participating in a fundamental problematic of modern thought, that of the "being man as subject," moving "toward the very interesting 'object in himself' (*zurück zum Gegenstand*)." The dynamic ensemble "the man acts" is for him an *experience* that unveils both "conscious liberty" [*liberté consciente*] and "efficient consciousness" [*conscience efficiente*]. But, after having defined the "transcendence of the person in the act" as an "active domination" and a "self-possession" linked to self-determination or to the will, he adds a further aspect: "the integration of the person into the act." "Without this integration, transcendence finds itself suspended in a certain supernatural void" (216). And it is the "body" and the "psyche" that become the main actors in this further *integration* of *transcendence*. Not unaware of the "drives," and among them the "sexual and genital drives," along with the "characteristic somatic difference between man and woman" (247–249), the author recommends their "participative" mastery: "Man 'is' not his body, he 'possesses' his body" (234).

The moralizing drift of this "possession" is all too obvious. Still, the phenomenologist theologian announces truly libertarian openings that members of religious orders and politicians of all stripe would do well to consider.

First of all, this priority given to the "person" as the basis of the "community": "I personally consider that understanding the community and relations between people cannot be presupposed in a just way if this is not based . . . upon the conception of the person and the act" (337–338).

Finally, and above all, this standing up for active and visible singularity, face to face with pure metaphysical contemplation. To those who fear that "existential contingency" may take up too much space, to the detriment of the "ontic status" of man, the author responds, "The object of this study is therefore the person such as he reveals

himself in action—such as he reveals himself through all the psychosomatic conditionings that are both man's richness and specific
limitation. . . . It was a question of pinpointing within the experience
of the act that which bears witness to man as person, that which in
a certain way renders this person visible—it was not a matter, however, of elaborating a theory of the person as being, a metaphysical
conception of man" (337–338).

Is this, really, a religion like the rest? And to think that some
still try to "reconcile" faith and reason, Europe and the third world,
freedom and women in veils! Far better than some improbable di-
plomacy, here is a *recasting* already at work, with Husserl and Wojtyla
among others—and many others—in the indefatigable, interminable
questioning of the subject, of the person, of the act, of the drives, of
the need to believe, of the rights of man, and even perhaps—it's not
impossible—of the right to caricature. A recasting that opens the
way to an endless . . . recomposition?

"Don't be afraid of Christianity, and together we won't fear religions!" I find myself wanting to say to my agnostic, humanist, atheist
friends. We hail from the same continent of thought, we often rise
up "against" each other because we are in reality "right against" one
another; let us continue our analyses . . . And I have a dream: may
true complicities, essential in our face to face with the rise of barbarity, be woven not only, and to my way of thinking less, between
Christianity and the other religions today tempted by fundamentalism, but between Christianity and this vision to which I adhere that
grows out of Christianity, although it is detached from it today, and
has the ambition to elucidate the perilous paths of freedom. In his
person and his acts Jean Paul II made this dream possible. Far more
than sainthood, this pope has shown us his universal dimension.

NOTES

The Big Question Mark

1. *Bisogno di credere: Un punto di vista laico* (Rome: Donzelli, 2006).

This Incredible Need to Believe

1. The interview took place on October 18, 2006.
2. Julia Kristeva's *Thérèse mon amour* (Paris: Fayard) was published in 2008.

From Jesus to Mozart

1. Interview with Claire Folscheid in *Paris Notre-Dame*, the magazine of the Paris diocese, March 16, 2006.

"Suffering"

1. This text is the fruit of a lecture given at Notre-Dame de Paris within the framework of a dialogue between faith and contemporary thought in which Julia Kristeva and Anne-Marie Pelletier discussed

the theme of "Suffering." This text was first published in the collection *Voici l'homme* (Paris: Parole et Silence, 2006).

2. "La mort et le bûcheron" [Death and the woodcutter].
3. *Entretiens avec Catherine II* [Conversations with Catherine II], chapter 2.
4. *Julie ou la Nouvelle Heloïse* [Julie or the New Heloise].
5. John 14:7–12.
6. Ephesians 4:9.
7. Ibid., p. 10.
8. Colossians 1:16.
9. Hegel, *Lessons on the Philosophy of Religion,* vol. 3.
10. Nietzsche, *L'Antéchrist* [The Antichrist], p. 40.
11. Urs von Balthasar, *La gloire et la croix* [Glory and the cross], vol. 3, 2, "La Nouvelle Alliance" (Paris: Aubier, 1975).
12. "Chant entre l'âme et l'Époux" [Song between the soul and the Spouse].
13. Proposition 36.

THE GENIUS OF CATHOLICISM

1. Text published on the occasion of the death of John Paul II in a special number of the daily paper *La Croix,* April 8, 2005.

DON'T BE AFRAID OF EUROPEAN CULTURE

1. Text published in *La Croix,* April 6, 2006.
2. Cf. *La foi selon Jean de la Croix* [Faith according to John of the Cross] (Paris: Cerf, 1980), pp. 33–34.
3. Cf. Karol Wojtyla, *Personne et acte (1977–1980)* (Paris: Centurion, 1983)

INDEX

Id, xiii, xiv; ideality and, 18–19; mysticism and, 11
Ideal Father, Christian Faith and, 49
Ideality: of adolescent, 16, 20; malady of, 16
Ideality syndrome, 17, 20, 21
Ideal Object of Love, 14, 17
Incest prohibition: society founded on, 56–57; Son-Father and, 60; unconscious and, 58
Individuation, 12, 13
Indo-European Language and Society (Benveniste), 4
Infantile polymorphism, 14
Innocence of suffering, 90
In Search of Lost Time (Proust), 35
Islam, 64–70; Aristotelianism and, 65; father role in, 66; monotheisms and, 64; original sin and, 67

Jean of the Cross (saint), 81
Jean Paul II (pope), 70, 87, 103, 106; genius of Catholicism and, 99–102
Jesus; see Christ
Jewish-Christian couple, 68–70
Jews: anti-semitism and, 71; Arendt on, 72–73, 74; assimilation of, 71–72; deportation of, 100; Freud as, 6; monotheism of, 67
John of the Cross (saint), 96–97, 101, 103
John Paul II (pope), 68
Joyce, James, 7, 85
Jung, Carl, 5, 7, 9

Kafka, Franz, 72
Kant, Immanuel, viii, 2, 17, 104

Klein, Melanie, 5, 39, 42
Kristeva, Julia, x

Lacan, Jacques, xiii, 5, 33, 53
Language: maternal passion and, 43–46; symbolic matricide and, 46; valorization of, 80
Law: holiness/goodness of, 31; suffering and, 50
Lectures on the Philosophy of History (Hegel), 33
Leibniz, Gottfried, 2, 54
Lenten Lectures, 77, 98
Literary experience, 29
Literature, 28; of Teresa of Avila, 51–55
Logos; see God Logos
Love: of God, 31, 89; God as, 56; -hate transference, 63; maternal, 43; of monotheisms, 64; psychoanalysis and, 62–63; quality of, 31
Loving singularity, of Christianity, 33

Man God, 88, 89
Masochism, feminine, 85; *see also* Sadomasochism
Maternity, 42; detachment-dispassion and, 43; language and, 43–46
Metaphysics (Aristotle), 65
Methodius (saint), 101, 104
Modernity, 29
Monotheisms: Egyptian, 66; Islam and, 64; Jewish/Christian, 67, 69; love of, 64
Mortification rituals, of adolescents, 19
Moses and Monotheism (Freud), xiv, 56, 66

Regression, 7, 19
Religion(s): clash of, 22–25, 26, 70;
    Freud on, 83; interpretation, psy-
    choanalysis and, 64; management,
    by borderline mental states, 8–9;
    power of, 23–25
Religious experience, 5, 36
Religious need, of adolescent, 20
The Remaining Time (Agamben), 69
Renaissance, 2, 20, 31, 33, 35, 36
Resurrected Christ, 69
Resurrection, viii, 31, 61, 62, 88,
    94–95, 96
Rolland, Romain, 4, 7, 8
Romanticism, 32
Rousseau, Jean Jacques, 2, 18, 90

De Sade, Marquis, viii, 2, 18
Sadomasochism, 55, 56, 67, 91; Chris-
    tian, 101; of mortification/peni-
    tence, 80; Son-Father death and, 61
Secularization, ix, 31, 71–73; of France,
    21–22; Shoah and, 13; uncertainties
    of, 32
Shoah, 13, 38, 71, 80, 87, 100
Singularity, 36, 37; of great men, 34
Society, incest prohibition and, 56–57
Son-Father: death, Christianity and,
    61–62; incest prohibition and, 60;
    sadomasochism and, 61; suffering
    of, 59; torture of, 50–51, 58–59, 66
Speaking being, vii, 28, 79, 80, 88
Spinoza, Baruch, 6, 34, 95, 104
"The Spiritual Experience in Dos-
    toyevsky and Proust" (Kristeva), x
Sraddha, x, 4
Subjectivity, original genius of, 35

Sublimation, viii, 12, 17, 34, 37, 42, 71,
    80, 89, 96; Christ and, 91; Freud
    and, 30, 60; Jean Paul II and, 100;
    maternal capacity for, 45; of sado-
    masochism, 56
Suffering: Beatitudes on, 81; of Christ,
    84, 88, 92–93, 95–96, 101; Chris-
    tian limits to, 82; Christian value of,
    81, 84, 91, 96; Christ's innocence of,
    90; divine and, 83, 96; law and, 50;
    Lenten Lecture on, 87–98; mean-
    ing of, 78–79; nihilism and, 79;
    psychoanalysis and, 77–86; recom-
    mendation of, 91; of Son-Father, 59;
    speaking being and, 80; Western
    tradition and, 79–80
Superego, xiii; adolescent and, 17
Symbolic authority, 19–22

Tales of Love (Donzelli), 9, 35, 42
Teresa of Avila (saint), 81; Catholic
    code of, 53; Christ union with,
    52–53; Counter-Reformation and,
    48–51; mysticism of, 47–55; Other
    immersion of, 53; pain as ecstasy of,
    97; visions/writings of, 51–55
Thomas (saint), 65
Thomas of Aquinas, 68, 104
Three Essays on the Theory of Sexuality
    (Freud), 13
Time, maternal passion and, 43–44
Torture, of Son-Father, 50–51, 58–59,
    66
Totalitarianism, 25, 72, 74–75, 97–98,
    100, 104
Totem and Taboo (Freud), xiv, 4, 9, 56
Transcendence, 25, 31, 104, 105

EUROPEAN PERSPECTIVES

A Series in Social Thought and Cultural Criticism

Lawrence D. Kritzman, Editor

Zygmunt Bauman *Globalization: The Human Consequences*

Emmanuel Levinas *Entre Nous: Essays on Thinking-of-the-Other*

Jean-Louis Flandrin and Massimo Montanari *Food: A Culinary History*

Tahar Ben Jelloun *French Hospitality: Racism and North African Immigrants*

Emmanuel Levinas *Alterity and Transcendence*

Sylviane Agacinski *Parity of the Sexes*

Alain Finkielkraut *In the Name of Humanity: Reflections on the Twentieth Century*

Julia Kristeva *The Sense and Non-Sense of Revolt: The Powers and Limits of Psychoanalysis*

Régis Debray *Transmitting Culture*

Catherine Clément and Julia Kristeva *The Feminine and the Sacred*

Alain Corbin *The Life of an Unknown: The Rediscovered World of a Clog Maker in Nineteenth-Century France*

Michel Pastoureau *The Devil's Cloth: A History of Stripes and Striped Fabric*

Julia Kristeva *Hannah Arendt*

Carlo Ginzburg *Wooden Eyes: Nine Reflections on Distance*

Elisabeth Roudinesco *Why Psychoanalysis?*

Alain Cabantous *Blasphemy: Impious Speech in the West from the Seventeenth to the Nineteenth Century*

Luce Irigaray *Between East and West: From Singularity to Community*

Julia Kristeva *Melanie Klein*

Gilles Deleuze *Dialogues II*

Julia Kristeva *Intimate Revolt: The Powers and Limits of Psychoanalysis, vol. 2*

Claudia Benthien *Skin: On the Cultural Border Between Self and the World*

Sylviane Agacinski *Time Passing: Modernity and Nostalgia*

Emmanuel Todd *After the Empire: The Breakdown of the American Order*

Hélène Cixous *Portrait of Jacques Derrida as a Young Jewish Saint*

Gilles Deleuze *Difference and Repetition*

Gianni Vattimo *Nihilism and Emancipation: Ethics, Politics, and Law*

Julia Kristeva *Colette*

Steve Redhead, editor *The Paul Virilio Reader*

Roland Barthes *The Neutral: Lecture Course at the Collège de France (1977–1978)*

Gianni Vattimo *Dialogue with Nietzsche*

Gilles Deleuze *Nietzsche and Philosophy*

Hélène Cixous *Dream I Tell You*

Jacques Derrida *Geneses, Genealogies, Genres, and Genius: The Secrets of the Archive*

Jean Starobinski *Enchantment: The Seductress in Opera*

BD
215
K7513
2009